30 DAYS TO
Taming
YOUR
Finances

1/2014

HARVEST HOUSE PUBLISHERS

EUGENE, OREGON

Cover by Koechel Peterson & Associates, Inc., Minneapolis, Minnesota

Cover photo © Photos.com / Jupiterimages; John Archer / iStockphoto

30 DAYS TO TAMING YOUR FINANCES

Copyright © 2006 by Deborah Smith Pegues
Published by Harvest House Publishers
Eugene, Oregon 97402
www.harvesthousepublishers.com

Library of Congress Cataloging-in-Publication Data
Pegues, Deborah Smith, 1950-
    30 days to taming your finances / Deborah Smith Pegues.
      p. cm.
    ISBN-13: 978-0-7369-1836-7 (pbk.)
    ISBN-10: 0-7369-1836-1
  1. Wealth—Religious aspects—Christianity. 2. Finance, Personal—Religious aspects—Christianity. I. Title: Thirty days to taming your finances. II Title.
BR115.W4P45 2006
332.024—dc22   2006004090

Printed in the United States of America

12 13 14 15 16 17 18 / BP-MS / 14 13 12 11 10 9 8

*This book is dedicated
to my loving husband, Darnell Pegues,
for his unwavering support of all that I do.*

Acknowledgments

It takes a village to write a book. This one is no different.

I am grateful for all of the wonderful people at Harvest House Publishers for their care and concern with every aspect of book publishing from start to finish. Their heart for excellence and practical relevance of ministry publications is unsurpassed. I am so honored to be associated with such a great company.

I want to thank the following people for their stories, comments, feedback, prayers, and inspiration: Bishop and Mrs. Charles Blake, Thom Singer, Tessie Thomas, J.P. Sloan, Pamela Johnson, Sylvia Gardner, Dexter Sharper, Sandra Arceneaux, Kelvin and Delisa Kelley, Alvin and Pam Kelley, Harold and Ruth Kelley, Carol Pegues, Janet Thomas, Creola Waters, Gina Smith, B.C. and Todd Talbott, Bunny Wilson, Dr. Barbara Young, Dr. Barbara Lewis, Judge Mablean Ephraim, Fayetta Tasby, Vincent Bussey, Billie Rodgers, Dr. Barbara McCoo Lewis, and a host of others.

To my mother, Doris Smith; my father, Rube Smith Sr.; and my six brothers: Bobby, Rube Jr., Dale, Reggie, Gene, and Vernon. You mean the world to me. Your support inspires me.

To all of my friends who patiently tolerated and understood my writing hibernation, thanks for being in my life.

Most of all, I thank God, who is the author and finisher of everything I do.

Contents

Prologue

Welcome to financial boot camp. I'm going to be your friendly drill sergeant for the next 30 days. I'm hoping you'll be receptive to my advice. I really don't want to drag you kicking and screaming down the road to financial freedom. During our journey, I'm going to ask that you address some issues that may have kept you in financial bondage. I will also candidly share my own financial trials and triumphs so that you may learn from my experience.

This book is not solely about spending less. Overspending is a symptom of a deeper problem. Rather than putting a Band-Aid on a cancer, we'll face some core causes. As you acknowledge underlying behaviors that have sent your finances spiraling out of control, it is my hope that you will be motivated to make whatever changes are necessary. The following brief chapters are not meant to be an in-depth discussion of the related subject matter, but rather a consciousness-raising effort that will cause you to look beyond the surface of financial matters.

Money is important to our existence. King Solomon, the sage of the Old Testament, declared, "Money answereth all things" (ECCLESIASTES 10:19 KJV). Indeed it does. While every *thing* you need can be bought, money is not *everything*.

Jesus made money a key topic in His teachings. Of His 29 parables, 16 dealt with finances and possessions. How we handle our money is a key indicator of our spirituality

Your finances may be out of control today, but you can decide now that this is only your temporary reality. If you faithfully follow the principles in this book, I promise you they will make a difference in your financial world. Get ready to receive the naked truth in a direct style that will challenge you to make whatever changes are necessary in order for you to enjoy the abundant life God desires for His children.

Day 1

Write the Vision

Write the vision and make it plain on tablets,
that he may run who reads it.

HABAKKUK 2:2 NKJV

Unlike the late Dr. Martin Luther King Jr., you may be thinking, "I don't have a dream." The truth of the matter is that everybody has a dream or a vision. For whatever reason that only you know, you may be too afraid to allow yourself to dream of what you'd like to see in your financial world. I can guarantee you that if you don't write it down, the chances of it coming to pass are slim to none.

Your overall financial vision, as God's child, should be to be an excellent manager of the money God entrusts to you. Your *goals*, versus your *vision*, are the long-term and short-term achievements you plan to accomplish in order to make your vision come to pass. Your goals should emanate from the heart of God rather than from your own fleshly nature or desires. So, before you etch your vision and goals in stone, don't forget to submit them to God. Invest some time in prayer alone and with another person whom you know to be sensitive to God's voice. "Commit to the LORD whatever you do, and your plans will succeed" (PROVERBS 16:3).

Don't make the mistake of putting forth your money and efforts only to find that you are climbing the wrong ladder to success. I am frequently reminded of the story of godly King Jehoshaphat, who invested hard work and capital into a shipbuilding venture that never got off the ground.

> *Near the end of his life, King Jehoshaphat of Judah made an alliance with King Ahaziah of Israel, who was a very wicked man. Together they built a fleet of trading ships at the port of Ezion-geber. Then Eliezer son of Dodavahu from Mareshah prophesied against Jehoshaphat. He said, "Because you have allied yourself with King Ahaziah, the LORD will destroy your work." So the ships met with disaster and never put out to sea* (2 CHRONICLES 20:35-37 NLT).

Whether written or not, plans are guaranteed to fail if they do not line up with the will of God. "'Destruction is certain for my rebellious children,' says the LORD. 'You make plans that are contrary to my will. You weave a web of plans that are not from my Spirit, thus piling up your sins'" (ISAIAH 30:1 NLT).

Once you get the green light from God, write down your overall vision and your goals. Written goals give energy. The more you read them, the more energized you become toward them. You need to divide your goals into two categories: short-term and long-term. The short-term goals represent what you'd like to achieve within the next three years. Long-term goals would be your desires for the period four to ten years from now. Prioritize each one according to their importance to you and indicate a specific date by which you plan to accomplish the goal. A goal without a due date is just a wish.

I have an acquaintance who asserts that she really wants to write a book. "I wrote three chapters about ten years ago," she moans. "I'll finish it someday." "Someday" is the date by which everybody plans to get in shape, pay off credit cards, apologize for bad behavior, and a host of other positive projects or dreaded necessities. Someday is no day. Every goal must have a milestone date by which something will happen that gets you closer to the end result. There is a line in the popular hymn "Yield Not to Temptation" that says, "Each victory will help you some other to win." These interim victories keep you motivated to keep going forward.

Here is a list of possible short-term and long-term goals to get you started:

Short-Term Goals:
I will save three months of living expenses
by _____.

I will quit my job and start a business
by _____.

I will eliminate all credit card debt by _____.

I will take a dream vacation to _____
by _____.

I will move into my own apartment
by _____.

I will complete my college degree by _____.

Long-Term Goals:
I will save $_____ for my child's college educa-
tion by _____.

I will purchase a home by _____.

I will invest at least $_____ into my retirement
fund by _____.

Even if you miss your targeted due date, the con-
sciousness of a deadline will give momentum to your
effort. Just keep moving forward. You don't have to
think of a zillion goals right now. Just start with one.
Succeeding at one thing can ignite your hope. Write or
type it in large letters. Start with the words, "By the grace
of God, I will _____ by _____." Be
emphatic. "I will" is more energizing than "I'm going
to try" or "I hope to." To stay accountable and true to
your goals, prudently share them with someone who
has demonstrated his support. Give him a copy and
permission to monitor your progress.

Again, I want to caution you that before you put
your goals in stone, it is important to ask yourself, "Do
these goals represent my vision or someone else's?" "Do
I really want to go back and get that college degree, even
though I am making good money, or am I just pacifying

my nagging spouse's desire for more social status?" If your goals are not God-inspired and ones that you can pursue with all your might, your motivation may wane and you may find yourself resenting the inevitable struggles—as well as the person who pushed you into them—when things get tough along the way. There are endless stories of people who went to college and majored in subjects in which they had little interest but did so to pacify pushy parents. In many cases, they are in unfulfilling, high-paying jobs and feel trapped because of their upscale lifestyles and corresponding financial obligations. Do the soul-searching before you even start.

You must be personally excited about the benefits of reaching the goal. Jesus was "willing to die a shameful death on the cross because of the joy he knew would be his afterward. Now he is seated in the place of highest honor beside God's throne in heaven" (HEBREWS 12:2 NLT). When Jesus died on the cross, He had achieved His vision. He said, "It is finished" (JOHN 19:30). Mission accomplished.

Day 2

See Where You Stand

Be sure you know the condition of your flocks.

PROVERBS 27:23

"You are here" were the first words I saw on a huge map as I entered the Las Vegas mall. As simple as it sounds, this was a very strategic piece of information. I had come to the mall with the goal of purchasing something from a certain store. I needed to assess my position before I could start on the path to the store. Otherwise, I would have wandered aimlessly, possibly become distracted by the merchandise in other stores, and may have never reached my destination.

Dealing with our finances works much the same way. Many of us put forth a lot of effort, but we end up spinning our wheels because we don't stop to take stock of our status. We are like the commercial airline pilot who, during a cross-country flight, made the following announcement: "Ladies and gentlemen, I have good news and bad news. First, the good news. Due to favorable wind currents, we are able to go faster than

See Where You Stand

usual. The bad news is that the compass is broken and we don't know where we are!"

You must determine where you are before you start to pursue the path to your financial destiny. To answer the question "Where am I?" you must look at two aspects of your finances: (1) what you own and what you owe and (2) what you make and where it goes.

The first aspect is addressed by completing a Statement of Financial Position or a Balance Sheet. See the form at Appendix A. This statement summarizes your assets and liabilities.

Your assets will consist of everything you own that has value, including bank accounts, paintings, jewelry, furs, collectible loans due from individuals, cash value of whole-life insurance policies, and so forth. You will list cars and real estate, even if you are still paying on them. Caution! Many people erroneously include the amount of insurance coverage on their term life policy. This is not an asset that you can redeem for cash today. It becomes an asset to your heirs when you pass away.

Now we will move to your liabilities. Here you will include installment debt, credit card balances, personal loans, home mortgage, and everything you owe. We will deal with how to manage your debt in a later chapter. For now, we are just going to figure out how much you owe. Don't go "ostrich" on me by sticking your head in the sand. Face the truth. Get your credit card bills and write down each outstanding balance. If you are pretty much maxed out on all your cards, don't worry; you have lots of company. Besides, I'm going to show you how to dig out of the debt pit.

For the second aspect, What do I make and where does it go? you will need to do a little more work. This information is summarized on a Statement of Income and Expenditures. See the form at Appendix B. Here you list all of your take-home income from various sources. You will list your expenditures in two basic categories: fixed and variable. The fixed expenditures are those that will continue to occur each month whether you have income or not—such as your rent or mortgage payment, car payment, insurance, and so forth. The variables are expenses that you can control from month to month. If your finances are out of control, there is a good chance that you may not be totally aware of how much you are spending on variable expenses, such as food, personal grooming, entertainment, and so forth. So, for at least a couple of weeks (a month is preferred), you're going to determine just how much you spend in the "variable" area—especially if you are making frequent trips to the automated teller machine and spending primarily by cash.

To make this a little easier for you, I have included in Appendix C a worksheet to help you monitor your spending. Write down every variable expense you incur for seven days at a time for four weeks. You can summarize the spending categories later. This process may seem cumbersome, but it's going to pay off. By making this short-term investment of time in seeing where your money is going, you will be armed with information that will allow you to control your spending in the long-term. So stay the course.

Again, I'm going to caution you to be really honest here. Some people sabotage this process by listing what they feel they should be spending vs. their reality. It is extremely important to complete this exercise because it reveals your real financial priorities, not what you claim they are. Imagine if I found your checkbook. Without being the slightest bit judgmental, I could conclude from reviewing it what your spending priorities are. So, again, just note the real deal. We will look at an ideal spending plan in the next chapter.

You do not need to attempt to make any changes in how you operate at this point. We are just trying to identify where the problems are in your current spending. You will probably be shocked to see where the money is going. Pay particular attention to the amounts you spend for lunch, snacks, newspapers, and so forth. I was really taken aback when my husband, Darnell, and I went through this process a couple of years ago and saw how much we were spending on eating out and for recreational-related items. My immediate response was to cut everything out—but that's not the best solution. Let's see what is.

Day 3

Prepare Your Plan

*Good planning and hard work
lead to prosperity.*
PROVERBS 21:5 NLT

Nelaton, the great French surgeon, once said, "If I had four minutes in which to perform an operation on which a life depended, I would take one minute to consider how best to do it." The adage may have become trite, but it is still true: *If you fail to plan, then you plan to fail.*

Now that you have determined where you stand, you are ready to chart your course—not to riches, but to financial freedom. Financial freedom is simply being free from anxiety about financial matters. Developing and implementing an effective spending plan—I dare not use the word "budget"—involves four major actions: (1) determining where you are currently spending the money, (2) evaluating your spending in light of your financial goals, (3) identifying and eliminating behaviors or circumstances that lead to unnecessary spending, and

(4) monitoring your ongoing expenditures to make sure they are consistent with your financial goals. You completed the first step in the previous chapter, so you are now poised for steps 2 through 4.

Whatever goals you set, your strategy must be designed to take you in that direction. For example, if you have a long-term goal of saving enough money for a down payment on a house, you cannot continue to purchase designer clothes on your credit card each month. In fact, your goal should be to eliminate as much credit card debt as possible so that you can improve your FICO score (more about this later), which will determine the interest rate on your mortgage, and have sufficient cash flow to comfortably afford the mortgage without having to take all of your vacations in the backyard. You will never get to the West if you follow a route to the East. Again, I challenge you to look at your goals in the previous chapter and see if you are ready to pursue a plan that will get you to where you want to be. We will devote the rest of this book to looking at what you should and should not do to bring your plans to fruition.

Because each person's financial situation is unique, there is no cookie-cutter budget that fits all. How you set up your plan is largely dependent on where you live, your marital status, and other personal circumstances. Nevertheless, I have set forth below some general guidelines as to how a typical plan would look for a person who is trying to bring their finances under control. For clarity, the example assumes a gross annual salary of $36,000.

Sample Spending Plan	%	Monthly	Annually*
Gross Income	100.00%	3,000	36,000
Shelter	28.00%	840	10,080
Tithes/Offerings/Alms/Gifts	11.00%	330	3,960
Short-Term Savings	3.00%	90	1,080
Long-Term Savings/Investments/Retirement	3.00%	90	1,080
Debt Reduction/Other	4.00%	120	1,440
Insurance	2.00%	60	720
Transportation	12.00%	360	4,320
Food	13.00%	390	4,680
Recreation/Social Life	5.00%	150	1,800
Subtotal Before Taxes	81.00%	2,430	29,160
Social Security/Medicare Taxes	7.65%	230	2,754
Federal/State/Other Taxes	11.35%	340	4,086
Total Expenditures	100.00%	3,000	36,000

*For ease of understanding, the numbers herein have been rounded.

You will need to consider each line item as it relates to your personal circumstances. For example, if you are married, have a roommate, or live at home with your parents, your Shelter costs may be a lot lower since you share them with others. You will then want to allocate some of the excess funds from this area to another category. Keep in mind that your Shelter costs include everything you spend money on to live in your dwelling: utilities, phone, maintenance, and so forth.

As you reviewed the sample budget above, I'm sure

that you noted that the Tithe, Offerings, Alms, and Gifts category appears to take a significant chunk out of your available funds. In the next chapter, we will look at whether this is something you should eliminate for now until you get your financial house in order.

As you move to the Short-Term Savings category, your ultimate goal here should be to save at least a couple months' take-home pay. In the scenario on page 20, saving $90 per month is not going to get you there anytime soon. In fact, at this rate, it would take 54 months to save $4,860. Clearly, you will need to reduce another expense category to achieve your goal more quickly.

The Long-Term Savings category assumes that you work for an employer who puts at least three percent of your gross salary into a retirement plan and that you will match it. We will deal with savings and other aspects of your plan in other chapters.

One thing to keep in mind is that your spending plan should not be viewed as a downward spiral of deprivation. It is extremely important to build in recreation and fun. We should not spend all of our efforts trying to make sure we have a good life only in the future. While we need to be wise today, tomorrow is not promised to anybody.

I want to caution that it is going to be a lot harder to implement the monitoring of your ongoing expenditures if you do not have an effective system for doing so. And I can almost guarantee that anyone who does not maintain a checking account, but rather cashes his check and pays his bills in cash, will always be financially challenged (read "broke").

There are some wonderful user-friendly software programs on the market that will not only facilitate the writing of checks, but also make tracking your finances a cinch. At the push of a button, these programs will give you a complete report of income and expenditures by category. Software such as Quicken is available at most computer and office supply stores at a rather low cost. It also allows you to set up your spending plan and track your actual expenditures against it.

Of course, if you are not computer literate and you want a super simple plan for tracking your expenses, put your budgeted amount of cash for each category in letter-size envelopes for the entire pay period. For example, "Lunch" is budgeted at $25. Put the $25 in the envelope. When it is gone, no more eating. Or you may choose to borrow from another category and sacrifice accordingly.

Now that you have prepared your plan, it is time to work it. The plan that you set will determine the quality of your life both now and in the future.

Day 4

Fund Firstfruits First

Honor the LORD with your possessions,
and with the firstfruits of all your increase.

PROVERBS 3:9 NKJV

I've seen many people attempt to put God on a shelf with the intention of entering or resuming a financial relationship with Him once everything is in place. This is ridiculous because, when all is said and done, the essence of a financial plan is to determine the best way, as a manager, to handle God's money that He has entrusted to you. The real issue is not how much of your money you plan to give to God, but rather how much of His money you will keep for yourself.

Tithes

The top priority in a God-honoring financial strategy is to address your obligation to Him through the paying of your tithe. The tithe is the first ten percent of your income. Many people debate whether tithing is strictly an Old Testament law that became obsolete.

Some have even said that we cannot use Jesus' words in Matthew 23:23 as justification for tithing in the New Testament.

> *How terrible it will be for you teachers of religious law and you Pharisees. Hypocrites! For you are careful to tithe even the tiniest part of your income, but you ignore the important things of the law—justice, mercy, and faith.* You should tithe, yes, *but you should not leave undone the more important things* (MATTHEW 23:23 NLT, EMPHASIS ADDED).

If Jesus says I "should" do something, I don't think that I should debate the issue.

If you are one of those people who say you cannot afford to tithe, I want to tell you why this may be so. You may not have made this act of worship the top priority in your finances. What you are really saying is that by the time you pay all of your bills and other priorities, nothing is left over. Well, dear friend, God does not want what's left, He wants what's right. You can always afford anything that comes off the top.

I'm totally convinced that God has been faithful in making provisions for me because I have been faithful in paying my tithes. In our 26 years of marriage, Darnell and I have never missed paying our tithes. We know this is a miracle in itself as there have been several times when it looked as though we needed the money to close the financial gap on a transaction or for other purposes.

But we just stayed the course and never stopped taking it off the top.

I view my tithes the same way that I view my car insurance premiums. The state of California requires that every vehicle owner purchase insurance. Paying for the coverage is in the best interest of the owner, for it protects him against loss. When one has obeyed the law and secured the required insurance, he can rest assured that he will not lose everything he owns if he should have a car accident. In the same way, when I pay my tithe, I am insuring myself against lack. Because I have fulfilled the requirement, I rest assured that God has me covered financially.

> *"Bring all the tithes into the storehouse so there will be enough food in my Temple. If you do," says the* LORD *Almighty, "I will open the windows of heaven for you. I will pour out a blessing so great you won't have enough room to take it in! Try it! Let me prove it to you!"* (MALACHI 3:10 NLT).

If you are a tither and are still struggling, I believe you need to look at all 30 chapters in this book to see how you may be contributing to your dilemma by not handling the remaining 90 percent according to biblical principles. God challenges us to put Him to the test—even when you have very little. Look at what He did for the widow who shared the very last of her food supplies with the prophet Elijah. "She did as Elijah said, and she and Elijah and her son continued to eat from her supply of flour and oil for many days. For no matter how much they used, there was always enough left in the containers, just as the LORD had promised through Elijah" (1 Kings 17:15-16 NLT). God rewards obedience.

Another question that frequently comes up is whether you should tithe on net or gross income. I believe we should tithe on our gross income because our taxes and other deductions are obligations just as our tithes are to God. If you run a business, however, then your tithe should be based upon the gross amount that benefits you (your increase) rather than the business' gross income before deduction of employee salaries and other business expenses.

Billionaire Oprah Winfrey says she paid her tithes when her income was only $10,000 annually. I began paying my tithe when I received $10 per month as an allowance from my dad during my early college years. Today, Darnell and I tithe regularly, and it is our privilege to also make sacrificial contributions to special projects and other needs of the church. I am so grateful that my spiritual mentors taught me to tithe early in my life. I believe it is much harder to begin tithing when you are making a big salary than when the tithe is small. Satan will always magnify the amount and try to convince you that it is too much money to just give away. Whatever I receive, I know that at least 10 percent of it belongs to God, and I make no plans to use that portion. Further, for unexpected amounts, I will stop and ask God if there is someone I need to bless. Many times He uses us as a channel for His resources. I heard someone say, "God will get it to you when He knows He can get it through you."

Offerings

Notice that we pay the tithe (or tenth) because it is required. A second level of giving over and above the tithe is offerings. An offering is like the tip on a meal in a restaurant. To say, "I'm just going to give an offering because I can't tithe" is like saying, "I'm just going to give a tip because I cannot afford to pay for the food." Along with our tithes, God expects offerings, evidenced by His question in Malachi 3:8: " 'Will a man rob God? Yet you rob me. But you ask, "How do we rob you?" In tithes *and offerings*' " (emphasis added). The amount you give for your offering and to whom you give it is left up entirely to you.

Alms

The third level of financial obedience is alms. These are the deeds we do for others in the form of money or goods. Some people think that they can distribute some of their tithes directly to the poor in the form of alms. Know that we are required to bring all of the tithes to God's house for its provisions. If you attend a church that does not help the needy, consider whether or not it is the place that God has called you to worship. Don't just decide that you will fix the problem by redirecting your tithes.

God sets a great store by alms. Proverbs 19:17 says, "He who has pity on the poor lends to the LORD, and

He will pay back what he has given" (NKJV). Imagine it. When you help someone in need, God in essence writes out an IOU. The interesting thing is that He never forgets it. He just keeps paying you back again and again.

Cornelius the centurion gave generously to those in need. When God decided to bless him and his household, He sent him this message by an angel: "Your prayers and gifts to the poor have come up as a memorial offering before God" (ACTS 10:4). A memorial keeps something in perpetual memory. Cornelius simply helped the poor, and God obligated Himself to pay him back.

Many years ago, my husband and I sent a very worn and worthy evangelist on a trip that we ourselves had long desired to take. Knowing she needed the rest and the serenity of that luxurious Hawaiian island, and also realizing she could not afford such a treat, we willingly sponsored the trip for her and her husband. Since then, we have reaped—and continue to reap—many wonderful trips from that seed. From luxury cruises at low or no cost to first-class excursions to the uttermost parts of the world, the Lord has demonstrated His faithfulness. I never fail to remember that each trip has been a result of that alms-giving seed.

If you want to make a difference in your finances, trust God and begin to pay your tithes, give offerings, and help the poor. You really can't beat God at giving.

Day 5

Save Strategically

Ants are creatures of little strength,
yet they store up their food in the summer.
PROVERBS 30:25

After the 1994 earthquake in Los Angeles, I worked as a special consultant for an entity that provided emergency loans to people who had sustained losses. I was amazed to see how little cash middle-class baby boomers had saved. Many owned homes, cars, and pricey toys that carried huge corresponding loans. Very few had made any preparations for a disaster. Their lifestyle as the "now" generation was very evident. I was reminded of King Solomon's warning, "A prudent man foresees the difficulties ahead and prepares for them; the simpleton goes blindly on and suffers the consequences" (PROVERBS 22:3 TLB).

Some financial planners advise their customers to "pay yourself first" by socking away five to ten percent of their gross income right off the top. I take exception to this worldly, "me first" thinking. As we discussed in the previous chapter, you must first pay God His tithes and offerings, and then you can begin to address your short-term and long-term goals.

Your most urgent short-term goal is to provide for an emergency. Let's deal first with the issue of whether you should save money if you are head over heels in debt.

The fact is, everybody needs an emergency cash reserve. The amount of the reserve depends on your living expenses. Most financial advisors recommend at least six months, but let's get real. If it costs you $2,000 per month to live, I doubt you will save $12,000 over a short period of time. If you were that disciplined at stashing money away, you wouldn't be reading a book on taming your finances. You would have saved and paid cash for the things you charged. Notwithstanding, your ultimate goal should be to accumulate a minimum of two-months' cash reserve at some point in time—but not right now. It may be wiser at this point to have only a month's living expenses in a cash reserve. If you keep your credit card balances low or even designate a special credit card for emergencies only, when something unexpected arises, you can use this card—not to draw down a costly cash advance, but to charge needed items.

If the emergency need cannot be charged, then you can tap into your retirement account for 60 days without penalty. I am making a big assumption here that you are already participating at the maximum level if your employer offers a matching contribution to a retirement account. It is the best investment you can make. For example, say you gross $3,000 per month and your company offers a matching contribution up to three percent. This means that for every dollar that you put in up to $90, the company will match it. You now have $180 per month going towards your retirement. Why, that's an immediate 100 percent return! Without burdening you with more details, suffice it to say that you will have a handsome amount of money when you retire. If your company does not have a matching contribution plan, then you will want to set up an Individual Retirement Account (IRA). Certain rules and restrictions apply, but you really should get more information on this to see if you qualify for it.

Now back to that emergency loan from your retirement account. Be careful here. If you do not pay the money back within the designated time, it will cost you big-time: a ten percent early withdrawal penalty to the Internal Revenue Service and federal income taxes on the amount withdrawn. You may also have to pay state income taxes and a state penalty, depending on the state where you live. My husband and I made such a withdrawal several years ago to buy a house for my mother. We were well aware of the penalties and consciously made the decision because the discounted price of the house warranted it. Nevertheless, at tax time, reality set in and paying those penalties was a hard pill to swallow. I hate paying out large sums at once. If you ever decide to make a permanent withdrawal from your retirement account, you would be wise to send in the estimated federal and state taxes immediately.

Set up a plan whereby you save something each pay period. The most critical aspect of a savings plan is that it needs to be consistent. One of my former employers once set up a Christmas club. There was a certain lady who requested to withdraw the money at least five times a year. With one step forward and two steps backward, you'll never get ahead. Try to get an automatic deposit to a savings account. Putting the money in a certificate of deposit or other not-so-easy-to-get-to instrument is a great deterrent to just putting your funds in a checking account or under your mattress.

In terms of an overall savings strategy, the first priority is to establish a small emergency cash reserve. Then contribute the maximum amount you can to your company's matching retirement plan, pay down your consumer credit, accumulate a two- to six-months' living expense reserve, and invest in a home, rental property, or other long-term instruments.

Stay balanced in your approach to savings. Ants provide a good model. They are very wise in their fore-thought and planning. However, we are not to conclude that ants spend *all* of their efforts in the summer pre-paring for the winter. They do eat some of their food on a current basis, otherwise they would perish. And so it is with man. I have heard couples complain that a spouse just wants to save all of the money for the future with vacations being out of the question. This can cause a marriage to perish.

Speaking of vacations, what about that dream trip? Have you called the travel agency to find out what it will cost and how much you will need to put aside each month to accumulate the necessary amount? Or do you plan to charge the whole thing and spend the next few years paying for it? To accomplish any financial goal, you must have a strategic plan for doing so. Just make sure the plan doesn't destroy the quality of your life.

Darnell and I have an overall philosophy on how we handle our money: give some, save some, spend some.

Day 6

Diminish Your Debt

The rich rule over the poor,
and the borrower is servant to the lender.

PROVERBS 22:7

We are a nation of consumers with credit instantly available to help us gratify our desires and medicate our insecurities. Recent surveys revealed that the average American family spends 122 percent of their gross income and maintains average credit card balances of $7,500. Excess consumer debt is evidence that we are spending money we wish we earned.

God's position on debt is very clear. It puts the borrower in bondage to the lender. Debt is a subtle form of slavery, and He doesn't want His children living in bondage to anybody. When you can't even begin to dream about a real vacation because of your debt, you are in bondage. When you can only make the minimum payments on your credit cards, you are in bondage. When you can never make a sacrificial gift to your church building projects because of your debt, you are in bondage. In fact, many churches have to go into huge debt to finance their capital projects because their members are in debt. If everyone were debt free and embraced the principles of tithes and offerings, there would be no need to borrow.

While the Scriptures do not prohibit us from incurring debt, in each instance where debt is discussed, there is negativity surrounding it. Because debt limits our freedom to make choices about the rest of our life, it would seem wise to minimize or eliminate it. Our ultimate goal should be to become debt free.

That said, there is good debt and bad debt. For instance, a residential mortgage is good debt. When you purchase your home, you have invested in an asset that will continue to increase in value, stabilize your housing costs, provide a tax write-off, give you credibility, and become a significant factor in your retirement planning. A college loan is another example of good debt. By getting an education, you turn yourself into an income-generating asset that will, in the long-term, put you at an advantage over the majority of the population. That's why the people who extended you the loan won't let you off the hook—even if you file bankruptcy.

The amount you owe on your department store credit card is bad debt. If you analyze the items you purchased, they represent things you desired rather than things needed. In some cases, the balances on your cards include items you consumed years ago.

Auto loans are not necessarily bad, for you may need transportation to your job; however, if you purchase a status car that is outside of your budget range, then you have entered the realm of bad debt. Let's get real. A car, unless it is a classic, is not an investment. Investments are supposed to increase in value; the value of a car decreases when you drive it off the dealer's lot.

Having a fist full of credit cards may have been impressive at one time, but now it is irresponsible. You really only need to maintain one or two cards that you will use for additional identification or if you travel, rent cars, or stay in hotels. MasterCard and Visa are more widely accepted than others, so they are the recommended cards. You must learn to be smart in using your credit cards. It would be wise to use credit cards that offers travel miles or other perks for using them. Make the cards work for you. Use "their" money interest free by paying all purchases in full when the bill arrives. Even if you can't pay in full, at least make your payment as soon as the bill arrives. Don't allow the bill to just sit around waiting for the due date and collecting interest when you have adequate funds available to make the payment. The sooner the bank gets your check, the less interest you pay. Do whatever is necessary to avoid delinquencies. We will look at how your payment history impacts your FICO score in a later chapter.

A complete understanding of the real cost of using a credit card may be enough to help you avoid the plastic. Appendix E presents a scenario of a $5,000 purchase. The "victim" chose only to make the minimum payment on the bill each month. It appeared that the credit card company was being really nice in lowering the minimum payment each month to 2.5 percent of the outstanding balance. The truth of the matter is that this strategy is designed to increase the length of time that the debt is outstanding so that the bank earns more interest. In our example, the customer bought the bait and took more than 26 years to pay off the balance.

It really isn't that hard to get out of debt once you decide to allow the grace of God to help you to discipline yourself to do what's needed. If you think about it, you already exercise discipline in many areas of your life. For example, do you take care of your hygiene needs daily? Do you go to work each day? Do you refrain from speeding when you see a police car? The fact is, there would be negative consequences in each of these instances if you failed to discipline yourself. The problem with incurring debt is that the consequence is not immediate—it takes several days or weeks before a payment is required. Before you plop down that plastic, ask yourself, "If I had to go to the bank and apply for a loan to pay for this, would I buy it?" Well, credit cards are nothing more than preapproved, high-interest bank loans. If you charge anything and cannot pay it in full when the bill comes, consider yourself in trouble—unless you are deliberately trying to build a credit history by showing that you can make monthly payments. Even so, keep the funds in reserve to pay the amount in full.

Consolidating your debt into one payment may sound like a bright idea—especially if you obtain a home equity loan to do so. You will pay a lot less interest on a home equity loan than you would on each credit card. Plus, the interest becomes tax deductible up to a certain limit. However, you now have a greater potential for getting into even more debt because you have paid off those credit card balances. If you don't cut the cards up or hand them over to a trusted friend, you could find yourself in an even deeper hole, and now your house is on the line.

Let's look at a simple plan for digging out of debt. Start with the debt that has the lowest balance. This is the one you will pay off first. Why? It will free up cash sooner to apply to remaining debts. You will feel a sense of accomplishment once a single debt has been totally eliminated, and will have greater incentive to keep up the good work. While you are paying it off, add an extra amount to the minimum monthly payment. Where do you find the "extra amount"? Try taking your lunch and snacks to work three days a week. This may yield an extra $50 per month. And do you really *need* all of those extra telephone services?

Continue paying the minimum payment on all other debts until the smallest debt is paid off. When this debt is paid in full, take the amount (the minimum plus the extra payment you have been paying) and add it to the minimum payment on debt number two.

If you faithfully follow this strategy, you will turbo charge your way out of debt in remarkable time. Decide now what you will do with the money once all of the debt is paid off. This is not the time to celebrate with a spending spree. Try finding another way to reward yourself. I presented this strategy at a women's conference several years ago. I asked the ladies to stop going into debt to buy new outfits for the conference. The next year, one of the participants came up to me beaming. "I followed your principles," she said, "and I am debt free. I didn't buy new clothes for the conference this year. I feel such freedom!" I am always amazed at women who come to a conference from afar but feel that the other women, whom they don't even know, will somehow sense a previously worn garment and judge them for wearing it. Thank God for those who have found freedom from this debt-generating mind-set.

It's important not to put yourself in a position where you will be tempted to incur additional debt. The apostle Paul warned, "Make no provision for the flesh, to fulfill its lusts" (ROMANS 13:14 NKJV). If you still frequent the mall, even for an occasional walk, you are making provision to fulfill your shopping desire. It is like putting mice in charge of the cheese. To minimize your risk, take only enough money to the mall to buy the necessity that caused you to go there.

Make every effort to get and stay out of debt. You can't begin to plan for investments that may yield a 5 to 15 percent return when you are burdened with debt costing you 18 to 22 percent. Do the math. Know that the same power that gives you discipline in other areas can help you in managing your debts.

And don't try to do it alone; seek God's help.

Day 7

Ask for What You Want

Ye have not, because ye ask not.

JAMES 4:2 KJV

It's hard to receive some things if you don't ask for them. Asking can sometimes be scary—especially if the thing you request is for a benefit or a concession that is not normally granted. Even if most people attempt to ask, they will retreat at the first hint of resistance. The worst that could happen is that someone will say no—in which case you are right back where you started. If you are trying to rein in your finances, you will eventually need favor from somebody. Favor can bring you to a place that money could never buy.

I recently received a phone call from my friend Fayetta, who was bursting with excitement about the favor she had just been granted regarding her 30-year-old refrigerator. She was smart enough to purchase the extended warranty; however, the technician's last two attempts to repair the unit had failed. All of her food in the freezer was ruined as a result, and she was left without the use of the appliance for almost a month. She called the store where she had purchased it and boldly asked to be reimbursed for the value of the lost food. They agreed to that. She also asked them to give her the cash value of the repair so that she could apply it toward the purchase of a new refrigerator. The answer to that request was no because that is not how most warranties work. Now, Fayetta is very persistent, and she has a policy that at least three people must tell her no before she thinks of giving up. She kept going up the chain of authority and finally found someone who was not only willing to listen to her proposal, but decided to give her the full replacement value. Because there were no recent models to compare it to, she was given a completely new, upgraded refrigerator—delivery charges included—without paying a single cent.

Asking for favor is a biblical principle that most of us are reluctant to apply on a daily basis. God often gives us favor without our having to ask for it. However, there are times when some things will not come into fruition until we let our request be made known. The story of the five daughters of Zelophehad (NUMBERS 27:1-11) is a great example of how it pays to ask for what you want. Because their father had died in the wilderness and they had no brothers, they asked Moses to grant them their father's portion of the property in the Promised Land. At that time, only men could inherit land. God gave Moses the okay, and he not only granted their request, but also changed the laws for future generations of women who would find themselves in similar circumstances. You must not assume that anyone is going to have as great a concern for your finances as you. You must be proactive in getting what you want.

Jesus encouraged His disciples to be persistent in prayer by giving them an example of a man who had unexpected guests arrive and he had no bread to give them. He went to his friend's house quite late at night and asked for three loaves. Since the friend and his family were already in bed, the friend told him to come back tomorrow. However, the man was not to be deterred. He kept asking until he wearied his friend. Jesus concluded the parable by giving the moral of the story. "I say to you, though he will not rise and give to him because he is his friend, yet because of his persistence he will rise and give him as many as he needs" (LUKE 11:8 NKJV).

Why are some people reluctant to ask for favor? Do they feel that others will resent them if they get an unfair advantage? Are they afraid that the person whom they are asking will no longer like them or will see them as a troublemaker? Do they fear being perceived as someone who does not want to work or pay for every single thing they obtain? Is their self-esteem so low that they feel they do not deserve favorable treatment from anyone? Are they such control freaks that they feel a favor will put them in debt to someone?

I'm amused by people who always want to be on the giving end but cannot receive from others. When I had this mind-set, I realized that subconsciously I liked having people feel as though they owed me something. It kept them in relational debt to me. If they repaid me by giving me something back, that made us even and I no longer held the advantage in the relationship. This way of thinking is very subtle and often denied, but when you let God shine the light on your heart, you can be healed of your controlling ways and will find it easier to receive from others.

I make every effort to plant the seeds of favor in whatever way I can. I have often provided financial consulting for free or at super discounted rates for those who could not afford it—or even those who could. Further, I share information and professional contacts with people who would be considered as competitors. I have also learned not to protest when I receive favor in return. I simply acknowledge it as a manifestation of the Word of God: "Give, and it shall be given unto you; good measure, pressed down, and shaken together, and running over, shall men give into your bosom" (LUKE 6:38 KJV).

When I was awarded a fellowship to pursue a postgraduate degree, I asked the private foundation that had granted my undergraduate student loan to defer payments until I graduated. They agreed and waived additional interest charges to boot. Favor, favor.

Is there a financial favor that you need to ask for today? Do you need someone to reduce an outstanding debt? To extend a start-up loan for your new business? To give you a concession on car repairs? To waive delivery charges on a major purchase? To defer payments without it showing up on your credit? To babysit your children at a minimal cost?

Well, are you righteous; that is, in right standing with your heavenly Father? If so, then expect favor. You're surrounded with it! "For surely, O LORD, you bless the righteous; you surround them with your favor as

with a shield" (PSALM 5:12). Be bold and expect a yes!
Caution. When "no" is the final answer to your persistence, submit your desires to God's sovereign plan. He
is working out something better. Stay sensitive to His
Spirit, and remember that no one can thwart God's
purpose for your life (ISAIAH 14:27).

Day 8

Investigate Your Insurance

A prudent person foresees the danger ahead and
takes precautions; the simpleton goes blindly
on and suffers the consequences.

PROVERBS 22:3 NLT

Perhaps you've heard someone remark, "Buying
insurance is not biblical. After all, Jesus told His disciples not to worry about tomorrow." Well, let's take a
good look at that statement.

> *Then Jesus said to his disciples: "There-*
> *fore I tell you, do not worry about your life,*
> *what you will eat; or about your body, what*
> *you will wear. Life is more than food, and*
> *the body more than clothes. Consider the*
> *ravens: They do not sow or reap, they have*
> *no storeroom or barn; yet God feeds them.*
> *And how much more valuable you are than*
> *birds!"* (LUKE 12:22-24).

Jesus was cautioning His followers not to be anxious
about the basic necessities of life—food and clothes. He

was not giving them a license to practice poor stewardship over what their heavenly Father had entrusted to
them. He was assuring them that if God created them,
He was obligated to care for them. God knew that things
would happen that would be outside of our control. He
also knew we could minimize our financial losses by
insuring against some of them where possible. Let's look
at some areas of insurance where we, as good stewards,
should focus or refocus our attention.

Life Insurance

There are basically two types of life insurance that
you can buy: whole-life and term. If you have a whole-
life insurance policy, it is not the wonderful investment
the insurance salesman told you it was. The company
takes your premiums, buys a certain amount of insurance coverage, and invests the difference in some low-
return investment. After several years, the investment
builds up to a "cash value," and you can borrow against
it or cancel the policy and take it directly. During the
early years of the policy, a huge portion of your premiums goes to the salesman as a commission. The plus
side of whole-life insurance is that you are covered for
your whole life, even when you reach the point where
you do not necessarily need insurance—when you have
no more dependents or anybody who will need your
money to survive and you have enough money in the
bank to pay for your funeral. The premiums on whole-
life insurance are a lot higher than they would be for
the same coverage on a term policy. In fact, you could

get even more coverage on a term policy for the same amount of money.

But hold on a minute. If you are 50 or older or if you smoke or have a serious preexisting medical condition, don't run out and cancel your whole-life policy. You may not be able to find a company to write you a term policy. Having heard me teach this in a seminar, one lady made an irate call to her whole-life agent for not exposing her to the benefits of term life insurance. She was ready to dump the policy without securing the term coverage first. Do your homework and call several life insurance companies and find out what their rates would be for a term policy. And remember that these policies only cover a certain length of time, such as five to thirty years. Buy coverage for a length of time that fits your need or desire. For example, if you are single and have a 15-year-old, you may want to make sure that if you were to die in the next ten years, you would leave him enough to cover his expenses until he is 25. After that, you may decide he has to fend for himself. Therefore, you would buy a ten-year policy. If you die after the term of the policy, too bad! No coverage.

Private Mortgage Insurance

If you purchased a home several years ago and paid less than 20 percent down, your lender surely required you to purchase private mortgage insurance (PMI)—not to protect you or the house, but to cover them in case something happens to you and they have to sell the house at a discount plus other expenses. However, you may be able to get out of this insurance. Here's how. Simply divide your outstanding mortgage balance by the original purchase price of the house (sorry, they won't use current market value). If the ratio is less than 80 percent, call the lender and ask them to cancel this insurance. In fact, if the ratio is 78 percent or less, the lender is required by law to cancel it—assuming you meet other conditions. Just in case they have forgotten, this would be a good time to ask them if you qualify for the cancellation.

Auto Insurance

If you live in a state in which insurance is mandated by law, then get coverage. God requires us to "submit to the government and its officers" (TITUS 3:1 NLT). Auto insurance will protect you, so don't skirt it. Do a lot of comparison shopping, calling companies known to offer low rates. A good way to lower your auto insurance premium is to go for a higher deductible. If you find that you simply cannot afford it, ask God to send the resources just as He did when Jesus instructed Peter to go fishing to find the exact amount in a fish's mouth to pay their tax assessment (MATTHEW 17:24-27). God has resources beyond your paycheck or other expected income.

Mortgage and Other Credit Insurance

If you bought a home, a car, an appliance, or any other major asset, you may have decided to buy credit insurance so that if something happened to you, the outstanding balance would be paid off. This type of insurance is strictly voluntary and is more costly than just buying a general term life insurance policy that gives your heirs the option of paying off whatever they desire. Why, they may decide it is not in their best interest to pay off certain assets, but rather to do something else with the money. My advice is to see if you can get out of the policy if you have this type. Caution. If you have a preexisting medical condition and can't get term insurance, then, as they say in the military, "As you were." Get or keep credit insurance if you believe you need it.

Other unnecessary insurance includes coverage for specific medical conditions, such as cancer. Unless the insurance company is going to give you a full rebate of your premium (mine does) if you have a checkup each year, then it's just best to insure your whole body and call it a day. If you are single without a care in the world and no relatives that you feel obligated to bless or support after your death, you only need enough coverage for your burial expenses—your job probably offers that for free. Why would you go and get a $300,000 policy, even if it is term insurance?

Buying appropriate insurance is good stewardship. We know God has us covered for every circumstance, but He has given us the sense and the responsibility to anticipate potential losses and to take precautions.

Day 9

Limit Your Luxuries

*I know how to live on almost nothing
or with everything. I have learned the secret of living
in every situation, whether it is with a full stomach
or empty, with plenty or little.*

PHILIPPIANS 4:12 NLT

"Wear the things of this world like loose garments."
These were words often spoken by one of my spiritual
mentors, the late Dr. Juanita Smith. The essence of her
warning was that we should not cling to anything so
tightly that we cannot give it up.

How married are you to your current lifestyle? Have
you enjoyed certain luxuries for such a long time that
you feel entitled to them? "Those who love pleasure
become poor; wine and luxury are not the way to riches"
(PROVERBS 21:17 NLT). If you are trying to tame your
finances, then it's time to distinguish between your necessities and your luxuries. You may indeed have to forego
a luxury or two in order to reach your financial goals.
Jesus let go of the luxuries of heaven in order to achieve

His goal on earth. "Your attitude should be the same as that of Christ Jesus: who, being in very nature God, did not consider equality with God something to be grasped, but made himself nothing, taking the very nature of a servant, being made in human likeness" (PHILIPPIANS 2:5-7). "Well," a certain man asked me, "that sounds good in theory, but how do I make it happen?"

First of all, it depends on how big of a mess you are in, how ingrained your luxuries are, and how badly you want to get on the road to financial freedom. Second, you must realize that you will need divine enablement to exercise the discipline to let some things go. Jesus reminds us that "apart from me you can do nothing" (JOHN 15:5 NLT). For every step you will take in your journey to your financial goals, you must stop and ask God for the strength to go forward. Here is how one couple got out of the pit:

> When we first got married 14 years ago, my wife and I were young and uneducated about finances. We both had credit cards with balances, car payments, and so forth. We had never really added up just how much we owed. Once married, my wife added it all up. Credit cards alone topped $25,000, about half of our pre-tax combined income. We set out a plan to pay off the debt and buy a house in two years. We cut way back, took no long vacations, and did not set foot in a restaurant for nine months. Others told us our goal was too aggressive, but we did it. Today, we still do not manage our

> *money as well as we should, but we have no*
> *credit card debt and we wait until we have*
> *the cash to make purchases.*

For this couple, long vacations and eating out were luxuries. I won't dictate what pleasures you should consider giving up for a season, but just in case you have fallen in love and married all of your luxuries, here is a list to consider: morning lattes from your favorite coffee shop, the daily paper, weekly manicures and pedicures, daily snacks from the catering truck, and bi-weekly golf outings, to name a few. Believe it or not, these items add up over time. I am not saying to eliminate them completely. I don't think total deprivation is a good thing because it can lead to a binge later. You only need to let go of these nonessentials for a season, or just limit your indulgence in them until your finances are on solid footing.

You can start now by asking God to take the desire out of your heart to spend money on things that are really just indulgences. The Scriptures admonish us to "love not the world, neither the things that are in the world" (1 JOHN 2:15 KJV). Your love for the things of this world will only fade with the help of your heavenly Father.

Day 10

Cease Comparing

You shall not covet your neighbor's house.
You shall not covet your neighbor's wife, or
his manservant or maidservant, his ox or donkey,
or anything that belongs to your neighbor.

EXODUS 20:17

Are you allowing your neighbors, family members, acquaintances, or other people to force you into a financial pit by attempting to match their level of material possessions? If so, why do you feel you must keep up with them? Besides, have you noticed that just when you think you have caught up, they go and buy something new, causing you to start a whole new round of spending?

Why not make a commitment to yourself that you will only buy what you can afford? Studies show that people who live beneath their financial means have longer and more fulfilling lives than those who do not. Sometimes the pressure to maintain a certain image or to live up to other people's expectations is so great that, if you are not careful, you will allow those expectations to force you to live above your means. To live above your means is to live a lie. A lie is any intent to deceive. Your attempt to deceive others into thinking you can afford things you cannot will keep you in a financial pit.

Further, comparing your material goods to those of others is a no-win situation. If you determine you have more stuff than the Joneses, you may fall into pride. If you conclude that your possessions fall short of theirs, you may envy them, attempt to catch up by acquiring more, and end up in the pit of debt.

One of my neighbors is a single, successful doctor who owns five Mercedes. Another neighbor has about seven pricey vehicles, a mini-yacht, a motorcycle, and a bunch of other toys. My husband and I have one car each. Does this motivate us to run out and buy additional cars so that we can be on par with them? Absolutely not. I have no desire to experience the "stress to impress" syndrome. Besides, having spent many weekends at mountain retreats, time-share properties, and places owned by friends and acquaintances, we have learned that we do not have to personally own something to enjoy it. We appreciate the offers to share our friends' blessings. We accept their invitations, thank God for His goodness to them, and rejoice that we do not have the responsibility of upkeep and maintenance. There is no need for us to resort to comparing and competing.

It seems that people who are always comparing themselves to others are getting their sense of self-worth from "winning" at this game. I know a young man, whom we will call Joe, who competes with a friend of his but denies that he does. When his friend purchased a plasma screen television, Joe purchased one that was a little bigger. Whatever the friend buys, Joe makes sure that his is bigger or better in some way. He never seems to settle down and savor what he has. Unfortunately, he also needs loans from time to time to catch up on his bills "until payday."

You would be wise to set your own standard of how much stuff and other pleasures you will indulge in. Ask yourself, "What do I really enjoy?" vs. "What must I buy to keep up?" I know a woman who buys fancy clothing for special occasions at church. All of the other women gather around and admire the uniqueness of her outfits. A few days later, her $10 offering check bounces. This is clearly a case of wrong priorities.

Day 11

Clear the Clutter

*Everything should be done
in a fitting and orderly way.*

1 CORINTHIANS 14:40

Have you ever felt so overwhelmed by paper and excess stuff that you wish you could just set a match to it all? I could say join the crowd, but the goal of this chapter is to show you how to leave that crowd. This is one problem you can start to eliminate today.

During a recent visit to my 75-year-old mother's house, I found the clutter in her drawers and closet indescribable. I decided that enough was enough. I went through every dresser drawer and tossed junk mail, pictures of folks she hardly knew, old Bibles with no covers, expired medicine, gifts she would never use, and a host of other nonessentials. When I reached her closet, I discovered items we had searched months for. I found at least four almost identical black skirts! I'm sure each had been a replacement for the other. And, despite the fact that we live in Southern California with its warm climate, several people had given her bulky fake-fur coats that took up the space of at least three outfits each and would have been more suited for life at the North Pole. I removed them all. I felt such a sense of accomplishment when I walked out the door. I also breathed a sigh of relief when she decided not to walk me to the car, since it was filled with all the stuff that someone less fortunate would soon receive.

Time after time when I have become fed up and decided to get myself organized once again, I always conclude my projects with the acknowledgment that clutter is costly mentally and financially. Let's look at some ways of dealing with this problem.

The key to clearing clutter is to begin with an objective vs. subjective attitude. This is not to say that you must completely divorce your emotions, for they are at the root of why a lot of stuff accumulates. Surely you want to hold on to things that memorialize key events and significant people in your life. But the truth is, even for key events you only need to keep a sampling or limited number of the memorabilia. For instance, you don't need to keep all of the leftover party tokens from your fortieth birthday celebration or the remaining 150 engraved napkins from your wedding reception. Just a couple or so mounted in a photo album should serve the purpose.

Now, to get you started, here is a list of things you should be able to toss without any stress or agony:

- Your report cards from grade school
- Your college notebooks

- Anything that has expired or is obsolete (warranties, insurance policies, medicine, old paint, carpet remnants [you've long switched to hardwood floors], and so forth). Keep real estate documents forever; keep tax records for seven years.

- Business cards from people you don't know

- Old grocery receipts

- Old magazines. Flip through one and see if there is an article you need to keep for an upcoming project. Toss or donate the rest to a hospital or doctor's office.

- Old novels. No need to keep for future reference; you know the end of the story now.

- Out-of-date, undersized, or oversized clothing. This can be really hard. If you have been holding on to an outfit that you dream of wearing, you may see this as an abandonment of your weight loss goal. You have to change your mind-set from one of "giving up" to one of "giving to" someone else's dreams. To ease the pain of separation, you might want to consider giving your special clothing to a nonprofit that you have personal knowledge of or one that directly impacts a select group of people you would love to help. Recently, I decided to give some of my never-let-go clothes to a women's transition home headed by a friend. It was so emotionally rewarding—plus I'm going to get a tax write-off to boot.

Clutter hinders your creativity. God may be trying

to give you all kinds of witty inventions and ideas, but clutter may be keeping you from focusing. It's like trying to paint a beautiful picture on a canvas that already has lots of other paintings on it. It can kill your creativity.

Make a commitment to allot an hour or so each month for clutter control. This approach has been very effective for me. I purge a selected section of my home office, closet, drawers, or kitchen at a time.

I have found that the real cost of clutter is time and money. When you have to work through clutter, it reduces the amount of time you have available for productive pursuits that could make a difference in your finances. I used to lose so much time looking for my car keys until I got smart enough to get a basket and set it by the door. Now my keys are always there.

Clutter also leads to duplicate purchases. I can't tell you how many times I have gone to the market and purchased items only to find that I had an adequate supply at home. The item was hidden behind something else in the refrigerator. My friend Sandra, who is a great organizer, arranged the food in my new refrigerator in a manner that lets me see most of the contents immediately upon opening the door. It is definitely easier to make a grocery list now, which saves me extra trips and the cost of gasoline to the market.

I have replaced garments I thought were lost at the cleaners only to find them hanging under other items. When I finally organized my closet with all of the seasonal clothes in one section and similar garments grouped together, getting dressed quickly stopped being such a frustrating task. Blouses were no longer hiding under coats, temporary hair (as in wigs) had not found refuge under hats, and torn hosiery was put out to pasture.

Have you ever missed paying a bill because it was lost under a stack of papers? This can result in unnecessary late fees that will ultimately impact your credit score. Do I dare mention the chaos in that cluttered catchall called a purse? Ladies, it is critical to organize your purse—especially the currency and change. I love those various compartments in roomy purses. However, rather than taking the time to put my money in my wallet after I had made a purchase, I would just throw it in the purse and let it land wherever. I have actually missed some great cash-only deals because I thought I did not have enough currency on hand and was nowhere near an automated teller machine. Later, I would discover I had more than enough hiding in all of the nooks and crannies of that bottomless pit. Once again, my disorganization negatively impacted my finances. I am still working on this one. Fortunately, I live with a wonderful neat freak who keeps me on track.

Day 12

Maximize Your Minutes

Teach us to make the most of our time, so that we may grow in wisdom.

PSALM 90:12 NLT

Time is just an interval on the continuum called eternity. If we really grasped the fact that what we do in this limited period will affect the quality of our eternal existence, we would behave a lot differently—not just financially, but in every aspect of our lives. Fortunately, time does not discriminate against anybody. Rich or poor, tall or short, we all get 1,440 minutes a day. The clock is ticking whether we are making the best use of the time or not.

Most of us have some sense of what we think is most important and where we should invest our time. Notwithstanding, I have found that many of our priorities exist primarily in theory. For example, you may say that your daily priorities are prayer, exercise, addressing your spouse's needs, and whatever else you deem important. But let's get real. Is this what you do the majority of the time? Write down what you do every hour for a couple of days. You may find that you often oversleep or run out of time in the mornings, decide to pray in the car, and rationalize that running out the door is going to be your exercise for the day. Our priorities are what we *actually* do, not what we *desire* to do. Let's see what we can do to change this.

Maybe you need to go back to Day 1 and write your vision for this aspect of your life. For starters, you can set up a simple prayer and exercise log. They are two different sheets of paper with the dates at the top and blocks underneath in which you indicate the number of minutes you spend doing each one. My exercise log, up until a few weeks ago, had lots of blank time. I was in denial about this, but the truth is that I had only made exercise a priority in my mind. I solicited the help of a very fit friend who is acting like a drill sergeant, and things are looking up.

I find that things do not happen if I do not write them down. So what about a daily prioritized to-do list? I mean, from the start of the day until the end. Now, if you are a type A personality like me, you will tend to fill up the sheet and stress yourself and everybody else out trying to accomplish the entire list. Trust me, this is not the best approach. So let's see what a sample day will look like and what might work for you:

To-Do List
- Arise by _____
- Pray _____ to _____
- Exercise _____ to _____
- Arrive at work by _____

- Tasks that must be completed (or started) today (list no more than three to five)

  _____

  _____

  _____

- Arrive home by _____
- Other tasks that must be completed at home (one or two)

  _____

- Watch TV or other recreation (yes, plan for some fun; but not too much)
- Go to bed by _____

Even if you do not own a day planner or a personal digital assistant (PDA), just keeping a record in a small notebook is better than nothing. Of course, I highly recommend the PDAs. Mine is essential to my daily effectiveness. The more unproductive time you spend, the less opportunity you have to maximize your time into a moneymaking opportunity.

Now that we have looked at what you wish your day to look like, let's look at some things you can do to make it your reality.

- Say no. "Yes" will bring you many friends; "no" will keep you sane to the end.

- If you have any influence, insist on an agenda (help to prepare one if necessary) for every meeting.

- Set a time to return all calls.

- If you are salaried (as in "I don't get paid for over-time"), set a limit on the excess hours you will spend at the office. For example, determine to work only one hour of overtime each day. Negotiate to have excess hours put in a time bank and redeem them later at 50 to 100 percent in the form of time off.

- Cancel your "open door" policy. Require appointments.

At-Home Strategies

- Screen your calls. Don't answer the phone when long-winded, whiny, or problematic people call you. Wait until you are doing something mindless (such as cooking or cleaning) to have a short conversation with them.

- Don't spend time arguing about unnecessary, non-eternal matters. Just say, "I don't share your opinion, but I respect it."

- Set a specific number of hours to devote to clearing clutter, working on do-it-yourself projects, preparing meals in advance, and other efforts that will save money in the long run.

Where we spend our time is an indication of what we value. It is most unfortunate when we allow others or circumstances within our control to dictate where we invest our time. We must remember that time is much like a coin. Once we spend it, it's gone.

Day 13

Spend Smart

Wisdom is a shelter as money is a shelter, but the advantage of knowledge is this: that wisdom preserves the life of its possessor.

ECCLESIASTES 7:12

Unlike smoking, drinking, and other bad habits you must completely eliminate to escape their clutches and consequences, shopping is necessary to sustain your daily life. Therefore, the key to keeping it from becoming a vice is to exercise wisdom and discipline in how you spend. Let's look at some common areas where you can be a smart shopper.

Electronic Shopping

Infomercials have seduced many into buying items that they do not need or use once they have acquired them. Don't be fooled by the convenience of ordering these items with their money-back guarantees and their 30 percent shipping and handling charges—which are never refundable. I have to confess that it was only recently that I overcame my weakness for exercise gear and miracle diet products or any other "breakthrough" merchandise touted on infomercials for three easy payments of $19.99 per month. The last straw was when I purchased a relatively expensive set of rubber-looking pots and pans guaranteed to perform better than traditional stainless steel. I never took the plastic off; they are still sitting there unused and taking up precious space. Besides, I have yet to order anything that performed the way it was advertised. I'm sure there are things out there that work, but I'm throwing in the towel on miracle products.

Pre-Owned Clothes

I know you are a King's kid, and the idea of acquiring something secondhand seems contrary to such a claim, but remember that we are trying to rein in your unruly finances, which in most cases got out of control because you were not applying the King's principles of money management. Buying brand new is not the only option. When God decided to bring the Israelites out of Egyptian bondage, He made provisions for them to acquire a quality wardrobe from their oppressors that would sustain them during their wilderness trek. "The Israelite women will ask for silver and gold jewelry and fine clothing from their Egyptian neighbors and their neighbors' guests. With this clothing, you will dress your sons and daughters" (Exodus 3:22 NLT). God could have easily dropped new clothes out of the sky whenever necessary. After all, He did so with their daily food supply.

Are you too proud to wear used clothing from thrift

or other secondhand stores? I know some pretty high-level folks who pride themselves on the deals they find in such places. Try the ones near exclusive neighborhoods, and you'll be amazed at the quality of the merchandise.

Basic Clothing

When you must limit your shopping budget, consider buying items that you can pair with other outfits in your wardrobe. Do you really think that it is wise to buy those hot pink shoes to match those hot pink pants? Why not try a black pair you can wear over and over again? Before you go shopping, do a quick inventory of your closet to see which basics (white shirt, black skirts, etc.) are most needed. If you must, you can buy some relatively inexpensive trendy accessories to spruce up your wardrobe. Just remember that next season they will probably be outdated.

Used Cars

I have heard many financially challenged Christians give testimony that, in spite of their poor credit history, God blessed them with a brand-new upscale vehicle from a very nice, sympathetic car dealer. What is not stated is that it comes with a large monthly payment that reflects an exorbitant interest rate because of their credit history, or an unusually long repayment schedule that is sure to guarantee the lender a healthy profit. In many cases, the exuberant recipient will have to exercise more faith to meet the payments than he did to get the car in the first place. What looked like a blessing is really a burden in disguise. I am often reminded that "the blessing of the LORD makes a person rich, and he adds no sorrow with it" (PROVERBS 10:22 NLT). Because a new vehicle loses so much of its value immediately when you drive it off the lot, a two- to three-year-old used car can often be a better investment. Of course, it goes without saying that before you buy, you will have the car checked out by a good mechanic.

Special Events

A good way to maintain a great social life at no expense is to volunteer to serve as an usher or to provide other support at various events. Just check out the social section of your newspaper and call the sponsors to see what help is needed. You'll get a chance to hobnob with folks with money. Who knows where that may lead? After all, God gives His children favor with man.

The advice above may seem a little out of your comfort zone, but remember that once you have stabilized your finances, built up a three- to six-month household cash expense reserve, and matched your employer's maximum contribution to your retirement plan, you can began to wisely add back some luxuries and acquire whatever assets the King allows you to purchase.

Day 14

Do-It-Yourself

*All the women who were willing used their skills to
spin and weave the goat hair into cloth.*

EXODUS 35:26 NLT

My brother Reggie is a real do-it-yourselfer. From
cars to carpets, his motto is "learn how to do it." He
repairs things that others would be ready to abandon
and makes them like new. My husband's motto, on the
other hand, is "call somebody to fix that." Well, if you're
of that mind-set but need to tame your finances and
make your money go further, it's time to dust off some
old skills or develop some new ones. You may even have
fun in the process if you keep a good attitude. Let's take
a look at some areas where you can make an immediate
difference in your finances.

Domestic

Have you fallen into the habit of paying others to
do your domestic chores and projects? My painter was
recently too busy with other customers to come and

paint a door for me, so I went to the home improvement store, bugged everybody that I could find, including another customer, and finally left with all of the supplies and how-tos I needed. I had never painted anything before, so I was a little intimidated at first. But the door turned out great, and the only cost I had incurred was for materials. It was a very rewarding experience. Further, I made a simple, no-sewing-required window treatment using yards and yards of rich-looking, but inexpensive, fabric. I have received many compliments on it. I'm ready to tackle anything now. I'm like the man who someone asked, "Can you play the piano?" He replied, "I don't know." "What do you mean 'you don't know'?" "Well," he said, "I've never tried." You'd be surprised at what you can do if you tried. Every day I am experiencing Philippians 4:13: "I can do everything through him who gives me strength."

Do you wish to spruce up your house but have no funds to do so? There is an entire television show and website (www.dyi.com) dedicated to showing you the details of every facet of remodeling and home repairs. Further, your local home improvement store most likely offers how-to classes.

Beyond doing home projects yourself, you could also decrease the number of times your paid domestic services will be performed by your providers. For example, why not stretch your housekeeper's service to every two or three weeks, or even once a month. You can change the linen, clean the showers, and vacuum the floors yourself. If you own a pool or Jacuzzi, request cleaning services less frequently—especially during winter months. And yes, you can remove leaves and cut wood.

Finally, do not forget to wash your car yourself. Enlist the help of your children, a relative, or a friend. What a great way to bond with someone. A thank-you, such as a sandwich or a few dollars, will still be less expensive than the price at the car wash.

Understand that all of these sacrifices are just temporary. You will be on solid financial footing soon and can gradually add back these services as your revised spending plan allows. The only goal now is to get out of the red and into the black.

Personal Grooming

You can save tons of money in the area of personal grooming without sacrificing your appearance. Pay close attention to the techniques used by your various service providers. Soon you will be able to do your own manicures, pedicures, eyebrow shaping, and other must-have services.

Day 15

Eat Economically

*A man can do nothing better than to eat and drink
and find satisfaction in his work. This too, I see,
is from the hand of God.*

ECCLESIASTES 2:24

Sometimes I wish God had made our bodies to require food only once a month or so. After all, He designed the marmot to hibernate for up to nine months. Imagine the time and money we would save. Now let's get back to reality. Since we can't avoid eating altogether, those who desire to tame their finances would do well to learn how to eat more economically. So here's my two-cents on eating in and dining out.

Make a List

You can avoid unnecessary trips to the market by making a preprinted list of the items you buy on a regular basis. Post a copy of it on or near your refrigerator. When you see that you are running low on an item, check it off. Don't forget to take the list with you to the store. After all my efficient planning, I would often leave the list at home. Just when I would start to make macaroni and cheese, there would be tons of macaroni but no cheese. Of course, neither to be outdone nor to waste money on gas for that extra trip, I used to get creative when I discovered I was out of one of the main ingredients in a dish I was preparing.

Pacify the Kids at the Market

If you cannot get out of taking the kids to the market, give them a "market allowance" of a couple of dollars or so to buy whatever they'd like. This is a great time to teach money management skills. Do not cave in to their begging for more money. Insist they spend within their budget.

Buy in Bulk When It Makes Sense

Some people take unit pricing to the extreme. They buy bulk quantities of certain items only to have them spoil because they could never consume it all before it goes bad. Don't be penny-wise and pound-foolish. On the other hand, large families and those wishing to be frugal would be wise to stay away from convenient individual serving sizes and items that have been pre-packaged. I love coleslaw, but I refuse to buy the little 16-ounce ready-to-eat package. Rather, I buy an entire head of cabbage and shred it with my serrated knife. This yields about four times the prepackaged amount at a 75 percent cost saving.

Cook in Bulk

In my effort to be health, time, and cost conscious,

each week I devote a few hours to the kitchen and cook several of our favorite entrees at once. I then put them in meal-sized portions in freezer bags. I have also invested in a food-sealing machine, which allows food to be kept even longer in the freezer. My husband and I can each take a serving to work for lunch or have it for dinner. We simply add a salad or other quick side dish. This works great for beef, chicken, and fish dishes as well as soups, casseroles, pasta dishes, and beans. Don't forget to label and date the freezer bag with a marker; everything seems to look alike when it's frozen. Also, since our dinner prep time is shortened, Darnell and I have more time to talk to each other—that rare pastime that few couples engage in these days. Of course, we still eat out one or two times a week.

And speaking of cooking, try to take your lunch at least three to four days a week. Plan to eat out only one day at a fun place. This really is a healthier and less expensive route. I priced a made-at-home, top-quality whole wheat turkey sandwich with natural chips and determined this lunch cost about 20 percent of the take-out version at a local eating spot.

Eating out is enjoyable, but it can really blow your budget. When eating out, try the money saving strategies below to tame the cost of this increasingly popular pastime.

Pre-Determine Your Ordering Limit

When I take my staff out for one of our morale-building lunches, I give them a flat spending limit to keep them from going overboard. Here is how it works.

To determine how much you can order before tax and tip, simply deduct one-fourth or 25 percent off your total limit. For example, if your limit is $20, take one-fourth off ($5) and limit your order to $15. When you add back the sales tax and a 15 percent tip, the total will be close to $20 without exceeding it.

Dine Early

Most restaurants will allow you to order from the less-expensive lunch menu up until late afternoon. This works especially well on the weekends. Call ahead or ask if this option is available.

Split a Meal

I'd say that 90 percent of the time my husband and I will split an entrée. Depending on the serving size, we also split a salad and certainly the dessert. You'd be surprised at how little it takes to satisfy your appetite. I'm just now getting it in this area. I was raised with a get-full, clean-your-plate mentality.

Stick to the Basic Meal

Skip the drinks and appetizers—unless you decide to make an appetizer your main entrée. Have the server bring it with the other diners' entrees or they may feel free to help themselves to it—after all, it is an appetizer.

Pay Your Share Only

Here is a common scenario. You enjoy the company of friends or coworkers who are big spenders and who always want to divide the restaurant bill equally. You normally sit there and stew because your share should only be $20, but it is now $50 because of their drinks, appetizers, and desserts—none of which you have ordered because you are on a budget or a diet. You do not want to appear to be a cheapskate, but these outings can cause you to blow your entire lunch budget for the week.

I am truly amazed at how much people will tolerate to maintain a certain image or to keep from appearing different from everybody else. Nevertheless, if the bill-splitting dilemma is a recurring problem for you, try this strategy next time. Ask for a separate check before the server takes the orders. If this is not possible because the restaurant won't allow it for large groups, ask for the bill when it arrives. Determine your share, plop it down on the table, and excuse yourself to the restroom. If you are really secure, forget the restroom and just explain that your financial consultant (that would be me) has you on a specific spending plan so that you can achieve certain financial goals. Don't assume that anyone will think less of you. You may start a revolution on how a few others will handle their finances.

If you really want to stick to your guns on this issue, leave your wallet in the car and only take with you enough cash to cover your spending limit. I've done this before. When they start the splitting routine, I'd say, "I just brought enough cash to cover what I knew I would spend."

Don't let this dilemma of splitting the bill cause you

to stop socializing with friends and coworkers. Just be assertive without any drama and keep having fun.

Ask for a Doggie Bag

Try to eat only half of your food and take the rest for a later meal. Your waistline will applaud you. Also, this gets you two meals for the price of one. If you do not eat the food within 24 hours, wrap it up and put it in a freezer bag for whenever you plan to have it. Don't let it go to waste.

Do the Standard Stuff

You know the rest: Don't go to the market hungry. You will likely spend more and buy things you don't need. I do this from time to time and often totally consume an item while shopping. When I get to the checkout counter, I give the clerk the empty bag, look straight ahead, and say, "Charge me for this." I would be wise to have a snack before leaving home.

And yes, clip coupons. They are available all over the place now—Internet, coupon books, mailbox flyers, newspapers. Keep them in an envelope in the car. Even if you are not a subscriber to the local paper, it's worth buying to get the coupons. You really can save a ton of money doing this.

You probably know most of the things I have suggested above, but sometimes it takes one more repetition of an idea for the lightbulb to come on and you finally say, "I'm going to do it!" So, as the Nike slogan goes, "Just do it."

Day 16

Restructure Your Recreation

They worshiped together at the Temple each day,
met in homes for the Lord's Supper, and shared their
meals with great joy and generosity.

ACTS 2:46 NLT

Recreation is a spiritual endeavor. In fact, Jesus was adamant about His disciples taking time to rest and regroup from all of their activities. I find it interesting that when they returned from their evangelistic tour and excitedly reported the success they had achieved, Jesus did not respond with an "attaboy" or a "keep it up."

"He said unto them, Come ye yourselves apart into a desert place, and rest a while: for there were many coming and going, and they had no leisure so much as to eat. And they departed into a desert place by ship privately" (MARK 6:31-32 KJV).

Jesus knew that if His disciples failed to shut down periodically for rest and recreation, they would become ineffective. We must stay on guard and understand that Satan wants us to go from one extreme to the other—all work or all play.

I observed during my years of financial counseling that women are more prone to overworking without recreational breaks than men. I'm guilty also. Further, when men play, they are more likely to engage in more expensive activities and feel no condemnation about the impact they may have on the family finances. Be honest. Are you one of these people who insist on engaging in "champagne" sports without regard to your "Kool-Aid" budget? Can you really enjoy only golf, skiing, boating, and other high-cost activities? Do you find the idea of eliminating or cutting back on these sports unthinkable? If you want to tame your out-of-control finances, then there can't be any sacred cows or off-limit activities. You simply must take a hard look at your spending plan and see how often you can reasonably indulge in these upscale activities. Keep in mind that you are a steward of the resources God has entrusted to you and that He will extend to you as much money as you prove you can handle.

I know a man, whom I will call Don, who played golf with the guys several times a week while his house was in foreclosure and he had delinquent outstanding personal loans. In general, his entire financial house was falling apart. He was frequently absent from work because of his recreational indulgences and was ultimately fired for his poor attendance. I can only explain his behavior as an addiction or just plain old irresponsibility. Whatever happened to jogging, bike riding, swimming, and other low-cost alternatives to pricey pastimes? Do you really have to meet your friend for breakfast, or would a brisk walk better serve you both while you catch up on what's been going on in each other's lives? For most of my close friends, I now ask that our get-together consist of a walk at the beach or around the local high school track rather than facing that irresistible basket of bread at our favorite restaurant. We save money and calories.

As you look at restructuring or downsizing your recreation, keep in mind that no matter what you do, recreation should refresh you mentally, physically, or both. The essence of the word "recreation" implies that new life is imparted in the process. Thus, your choice of recreational companions is as important as the activity. Engaging in pleasurable activities with pleasurable people maximizes the value of the recreation. My husband has made it his policy to try to play golf only with guys he really enjoys. He says that the camaraderie is an integral part of the activity. I have noticed that a walk with an insecure, competitive person increases my heart rate and puts a damper on my day. On the other hand, when I walk with a woman who loves God, who is pursuing her goals in life, and who knows how and when to listen, I feel energized. Many times the walk turns into a season of prayer or, at other times, just gut-level laughter.

Restructuring your recreation may mean that you pass up the popcorn at the movies. Did you know that movie theaters make more profits from concessions sales than from admissions? Consider making your own popcorn when you get home at a fraction of the cost.

This would also be a great time to critique the movie and to bond with your mate or date. After all, there certainly is no conversational bonding during the movie.

I'm sure you can name loads of things you can do to spend less on recreation. Take a moment and commit to at least one thing you can do right away. When you get serious about taming your finances, you will understand that change and financial discipline must extend to every area possible.

Day 17

Spend in Sync
with Your Spouse

*Can two people walk together
without agreeing on the direction?*

AMOS 3:3 NLT

Financial issues are the number one reason for failed marriages in the United States. Most couples would do well to understand the nature of a general business partnership and to model certain aspects of their marriages accordingly. For example, in a business partnership, the partners must practice full disclosure of financial information. There is no hiding of assets or details of transactions. Each partner agrees to the goals and objectives and has a say in all aspects of the enterprise.

When the Shunammite woman desired to build a guest room for the prophet Elisha, she didn't immediately call the contractors. "She said to her husband, 'I know that this man who often comes our way is a holy man of God. Let's make a small room on the roof and put in it a bed and a table, a chair and a lamp for him. Then he can stay there whenever he comes to us'" (2 KINGS 4:9-10). Neither the fact that she could afford it nor the fact that it was for a good cause kept her from acknowledging her husband. He obviously agreed to the idea, for the next thing that we read is that Elisha is settled into the room. What a great lesson for women today—especially women who command their own resources. Many feel that no man is going to tell them what to do with their money. What a relationally destructive attitude. In a business partnership, everything that comes in belongs to the partnership. Marriage is a partnership on the highest level. In marriage there is no need to track the contributions of individual partners because no one should be anticipating a dissolution or final distribution of these funds as in a business partnership.

Every couple needs to be in agreement on their major purchases. "Major" will be different for each couple because it is determined by their household income. Each couple must decide the maximum dollar amount that each may spend without consulting each other. Any amount above this will require complete agreement. Stick to what has been agreed. Trust me, this is important. If you do not get in agreement, should the deal go sour the tendency is to point fingers.

Many years ago Darnell and I purchased a spanking new recreational vehicle so that we could camp out with our friends. Darnell convinced me that it would also double as his regular transportation vehicle as he worked only a few miles from our home. Further, he sold me on the idea by rationalizing that since it could hold quite a few people, I would have loads of fun as he chauffeured all of us around town. We enjoyed a year of bliss with our new addition.

Things began to go sour when Darnell's company parking lot was demolished for a construction project. Finding a parking space on the street became more of a challenge each day. It was clear that he needed a regular car. As with most vehicles of any kind, the RV lost a significant chunk of its value right away. We had financed it and found ourselves owing more on it than the market value. The issue soon became, "Whose idea was it, anyway?" I silently pointed the finger. We sold it at a huge loss and chalked it up to experience never to be revisited—until we bought the "mini-yacht" several years later. I convinced Darnell that it would give me an opportunity to rest more and would even be a writing haven. Further, I would spend lots of time hanging out with him at the marina. He finally agreed. When someone warned us that "BOAT" stood for "Break Out Another Thousand," we laughed. It turned out to be no joke. By the time we paid the monthly note, slip fees, divers to keep the barnacles off the bottom of the boat, insurance, and never-ending repairs occasioned by our infrequent usage, we started to wonder about our own financial sense. Even though we both had been in agreement with the purchase, we apparently forgot to invite God to become a partner in the transaction. So once again we found ourselves owing more than the market value on a recreational investment. We threw in the towel and decided to sell. I am so gun-shy now that I am limiting my recreational purchases to tennis shoes and sun visors. The moral of these stories is to not only spend in harmony with each other, but also to get in sync with God. At least we can say that we didn't violate our rule for consulting each other on major purchases. It's just that we liked pleasing each other so much, we were not really honest about how we felt.

I have endless stories of couples that made big financial decisions completely out of harmony with their spouses. In one situation, the husband decided to quit his job for an entrepreneurial pursuit without ever consulting his wife. He announced his decision at a couples' fellowship as she sat there in shock and disbelief. She divorced him shortly thereafter. In another situation, a Christian man who runs a business with his wife admitted that he has misled her into thinking that they have a lot less money than they do. He says that she is too financially irresponsible. "Further," he rationalized, "I am the one who does most of the work anyway. She contributes very little." He feels he had the right to buy several expensive toys while limiting her to what he deems is a generous allowance. She resents him deeply for this. Rather than doing the difficult work of getting to the root of her financial irresponsibility, he chooses to deal only with the symptoms. The last that I heard, they were still at odds and smiling in church every Sunday as if everything were all right.

A significant amount of conflict could be avoided at the outset of marriage with effective communication about finances. Most couples just assume that everything will work out after they say "I do," only to discover very shortly that the response to certain financial issues is

"I don't." I believe couples that plan to have a godly marriage would be well served by having a good heart-to-heart conversation to make sure they share the same financial views and have put all of their financial issues on the table. Most find that this task has too much potential for conflict, so they avoid it. To facilitate such a discussion, I developed a list of 20 questions that are designed to focus on the most problematic financial issues that a couple will face. These questions are set forth at Appendix C, "Premarital 20/20 Vision Quiz for Financial Compatibility." Each person must answer the same questions to determine if they will have a problem with a financial issue. If you are contemplating marriage, then you must ask God for the courage to confront these issues before they arise.

If you are already married and experiencing financial problems, invite God to come into your partnership and give you the courage and wisdom to have "the talk." Start from the here and now; finger-pointing about the past will be a useless exercise. Bring everything out of hiding, including old, destructive attitudes. As you acknowledge Him in all your ways, He will direct your paths (PROVERBS 3:6 NKJV).

Pare Your Presents

*You must each make up your own mind
as to how much you should give. Don't give
reluctantly or in response to pressure.
For God loves the person who gives cheerfully.*

2 CORINTHIANS 9:7 NLT

It seems that there is always a holiday or special day of observance that requires us to buy a gift for somebody. My husband, though a very generous man, says it is a conspiracy of the floral industry. I have heard others say it is a creation of retailers. Whoever can be blamed as the source, we still feel the pressure to buy a present for the targeted honoree. Now, before you label me a miser, read on. When I reviewed our spending recap one year and realized how much we spent on gifts, I decided that it was time to pare down the spending in this area. As I looked through the list of recipients, I realized that we had purchased some of the gifts reluctantly or in response to the expectations of others. In particular, some of the wedding gifts were for people we hardly knew and with whom we had no direct relationship. Many of you have most likely found yourselves in this dilemma.

A few years ago I came out of the supermarket one night and was approached by two ladies who asked for directions to the nearest bus stop. Noticing all of the shopping bags they were carrying, I was curious as to how far they had to go. When they told me their destination, I realized it was not that far from my house and that it would be some time before a bus would be coming to the market bus stop. I silently prayed over whether to let complete strangers into my car. I felt at peace about it and offered to take them home. They accepted with great delight.

I found out they were both on vacation from Belize. I also learned that a majority of the bags belonged to just one of them. They represented gifts for people back home. The shopping queen then began to complain about the fact that she had to buy all the presents or people would really be disappointed because she always brought gifts back from the United States. She confessed she really couldn't afford them and was quite distraught that she was forced to continue this costly financial habit. Further, she had spent a significant part of her vacation time looking for the gifts and was physically drained as a result. She had started to dread the annual vacation because of this. There was no cheerfulness in her giving. I spent the next 20 to 30 minutes advising her on ways to get off of this roller coaster. Oddly enough, when I asked the other lady how she had managed to avoid this whole gift-giving burden, she simply said, "I just don't do it."

I have seen many people create a financial monster they never have the courage to slay. I am not recommending stinginess, but if you need to tame your finances, you must forge some brave, new disciplines. I know that for some people, especially those with low self-esteem, going cold turkey and just saying "no more" will be too much, so I'm recommending that all financially challenged folks start to buy smaller and different types of gifts. For example, in the instance of the Belize shopper above, I would suggest a postcard packet of Los Angeles's key sites rather than a T-shirt and cap.

Wedding presents for distant acquaintances could consist of a set of good quality white bath towels, sets of dish towels, a nice skillet, or other useful, generic items purchased from a super discount or closeout store. Forget about the bridal registry and the fancy place settings. This isn't mandatory. Also, forget about a cash gift. They won't guess that you only paid $10 for a $40 value, but a $10 cash gift looks (and is) cheap. If you stick to something useful, it will still be appreciated. Also, do not try to deceive recipients by putting the gift in a fancy box from an upscale store. They may attempt to exchange it, only to learn that it was not purchased there. Tacky, tacky, tacky!

Besides, what statement are you trying to make with your gift, anyway? Think about this long and hard and be honest. Are you living a lie by implying that you can afford such generosity? Are you trying to gain favor with the recipient? Do you know that favor comes from

God and it's free? "For surely, O LORD, you bless the righteous; you surround them with your favor as with a shield" (PSALM 5:12).

When it comes to those special days of recognition, you do not always have to send expensive flowers—except maybe on Valentine's Day (even then, your wife or girlfriend should understand a pared-down version). Focus on being thoughtful on a daily basis; that will mean more than a one-day obligatory observation. Valentine's Day is just a formality in our house. I am more impressed with Darnell's love for me when he insists on taking all of the grocery bags out of the car, washes dishes, fills my car with gasoline when it gets low, takes my car to the car wash, attends conferences with me to help promote my products, and shows overall consideration. To me, these are the best "flowers." Of course, being a woman, I do indeed expect *something*, but I am satisfied with a single rose and a card.

Speaking of flowers, a nice plant is appropriate in many situations and will last longer and may cost less—especially if you pick it up and deliver it yourself, which is a very nice touch in this rush-rush society. Why, I just recently threw out a seven-year-old plant that friends gave us for a relative's funeral. It was a nice reminder of his life. A floral arrangement would have wilted within days.

Other pared-down presents include white handkerchiefs for men, movie tickets, a magazine subscription, nice stationery, note cards, or a book. None of these gifts will send your budget spiraling out of control. In fact, I buy generic gifts (bath and body products, etc.), gift bags, and an assortment of special occasion cards a couple of times during the year and keep them in a special drawer. If I discover that I have missed a birthday, I can assemble an inexpensive, thoughtful gift bag in minutes. It really is the thought—rather than the thing—that counts. The important thing is that I remembered someone and went to some extra effort to let him know it. If a person can't appreciate a gift unless it is expensive enough to put in escrow, then I would question the authenticity of that relationship.

Christmas gifts seem to pose the greatest challenge—all for no long-term benefit. For instance, what were the three most memorable gifts that you received for Christmas last year? Can't remember? I assure you that the people to whom you gave gifts will have the same problem recalling them. So, if the gifts are not that easily recalled, why should you put yourself in a position of having to remember them each month when you make that credit card payment? Why give a gift that keeps on costing? Instead, give something simple from your heart. I was thrilled this past Christmas when a couple gave me a bag of personally concocted hot drink mix. They sealed it in a simple plastic storage bag and stuffed it in a gift bag with lots of tissue. It was so good that I coaxed them into giving me the recipe. I remember them every time I make the drink.

When you get to the point where your finances are stable and you are enjoying abundance, give according to your ability and your desire—and do it cheerfully.

Day 19

Further Your
Financial Intelligence

*Buy the truth, and sell it not; also wisdom, and
instruction, and understanding.*

PROVERBS 23:23 KJV

My brother and his grade-school-age daughter were
shopping at the mall, and she kept nagging him to buy
her something. When he told her he didn't have any
money, she innocently replied, "Well, write a check!"
Unfortunately, financial illiteracy is not limited to
small children. Senator Mike Enzi said it best in his
comments to the United States Banking Committee in
February 2002: "Financial literacy is something that is
needed over a broad range of income levels. No matter
how much one earns, money management is a necessity. It is something we need to begin emphasizing in
grade school and continue all of the way through high
school. It shouldn't stop there. Financial education
should be something we continue to concentrate on for
our entire lives."*

---

* banking.senate.gov/02_02hrg/020502/enzi.htm

Many times a person's finances have been derailed not so much from their disobedience to God's Word, but rather from a lack of knowledge of how to handle their money. I taught a six-week financial course for a small group composed mostly of young ladies who were college graduates. One of the students, bewildered by her low credit score, explained how she handled her monthly payments on her credit cards. "I don't pay on them every month," she explained. "I just save up so that I can send in a really large payment. Is that okay?" I wanted to faint! Obviously she did not know that her payment habits are one of the key components of her credit score. It is clear that many of our learning institutions are not preparing students for the real financial world.

If you think "points" are the positive benefits of buying a house or that an "impound" account is a cash reserve to redeem your dog just in case he gets caught without his tags, you need to improve your financial knowledge. Very few people invest in increasing their financial literacy. King Solomon admonished that we should "buy the truth...also wisdom, and instruction." It is extremely important that you empower yourself with some basic financial knowledge. Let's look at a few areas where this is key.

FICO Score

Knowledge is critical regarding your credit, particularly your FICO score. FICO stands for Fair Isaac Company, the entity that developed the formula that rates a person's creditworthiness. Every company that extends credit to you will use this score. The score goes up to 850. You will find yourself at a real disadvantage if your score is under 675. The higher your score, the lower your interest rate will be on your debt. The two most significant factors impacting your score are your bill-paying history and the outstanding balances on your credit cards when compared to the credit limits on these cards. For example, if you owe $8000 on all of your consumer debt and have a limit of $10,000, then you are 80 percent maxed out. This is not good. However, if under this same scenario, you have a total limit of $32,000 on all your cards, then you only owe 25 percent of what you could owe. Now this shows that you have exercised some discipline.

Your goal should be to achieve a FICO score of at least 700. How do you do this? First, check your credit report to make sure there isn't an error on it that is dragging down your score. Most credit reports will have some sort of inaccuracy. Second, pay your bills on time. Third, pay off as many bills as you can so that you can reduce the percentage of your total credit limit that is outstanding. Think strategically. Don't run out and cancel all your cards. Keep the ones you have had a long time (you need the history on your record) and just cut up a few excess ones. The FICO spy won't know that you cut them up; he'll just think that you are exercising discipline by not using them.

Car Leasing

In general, leasing a vehicle is usually not a good

idea. However, if you are either in dire need of a car and have no money for a significant down payment or you work very close to home and, on average, will drive very few (less than 15,000) miles per year, leasing is an option you may consider. Before you sign on the dotted line, ask the dealer for a sample lease and then let some knowledgeable person explain the terms—especially "guaranteed residual value." This is the value you are guaranteeing the dealer the car will be worth at the end of the lease term. Because this value is determined primarily by how many miles you have driven, you must understand that you can't just jump in the car and take a cross-country trip each year without penalty. My husband leased a car once, and we became prisoners to the odometer. "We'll go in your car!" he always seemed to exclaim. Of course, this caused us to rack up more miles on my vehicle, which we had *purchased*.

Business Deals

I advise getting professional help when you are about to enter a business venture—especially legal and accounting expertise. Uncle Joe may be doing great at his small business, but he may not have a clue when you start talking about the nuances of profit sharing agreements and exit strategies. Attorneys and CPAs are not experts in everything so get one who specializes in your area of concern. It will be worth the investment.

If there is any aspect of your finances you don't quite understand, then start asking questions. If you do not understand every deduction on your paycheck and know which ones are optional or subject to your control, then go to your payroll or personnel office and ask them to explain each one. You just may decide that you could improve the quality of your life by increasing your current deductions and taking home extra cash now rather than getting that large tax refund at the end of the year.

Keep inquiring, keep learning. "Let the wise listen and add to their learning, and let the discerning get guidance" (PROVERBS 1:5).

Day 20

Eliminate Emotional Spending

Why spend money on what is not bread,
and your labor on what does not satisfy?

ISAIAH 55:2

Emotional spending is first cousin to emotional eating. In both cases, there is a feeling inside that cries out for satisfaction. Spending to pacify an emotion is like getting an anesthetic but never having the required surgery. You get temporary relief, but the problem remains.

I'm pretty frugal, so I don't consider myself an emotional spender. However, after I have worked really hard on a project and I finally finish it, I feel I need to reward myself by buying something.

Let's look at a few emotions that may cause you to want to spend outside of your budget and a strategy for dealing with each.

Anger

If you peel the onion of why you are angry, at the core of it you may find that you are angry with yourself for tolerating someone's bad behavior, for not speaking up, for putting yourself at risk, or for a host of other reasons. Before you run to the mall, get in touch with why you are feeling the way you do and confront the people involved. If face-to-face is not possible, then write a letter expressing how you really feel about what has happened. Ask God to give you the words and the wisdom to be direct, honest, and godly in your approach.

Boredom

The best way to deal with boredom is to invest time in meaningful activity that either moves you toward your goals or makes life better for someone else. Take a class to enhance your skills or knowledge. Sign up with a group to visit nursing homes, hospitals, orphanages, and shelters. Go alone if you have to. It is so fulfilling to help others not be bored. Plant what you want to reap, and most of all, stay away from TV and Internet shopping, which make it so easy to indulge your fantasies.

Depression

I know I'm treading on sensitive ground here, but if you are depressed it may be because you have focused all of your attention on how things are affecting you. You have become the center of your world. If you would dare to step out of the spotlight and shine it on someone else, you will find amazing results. See the list above for possible activities that may refocus your attention. Notwithstanding, I strongly encourage you to seek medical attention to determine if your depression is caused by a chemical imbalance or other medical reasons.

Insecurity

When you feel unsure of your inherent worth as an individual, you may find yourself buying things that will impress others of your value. This can take the form of cars, clothes, jewelry, and other trappings. Some people can't afford to buy the real deal, so they buy knockoffs of designer merchandise hoping that no one will know the difference. They give the phrase "dress to impress" a whole new meaning. If you find yourself with this mind-set, admit it and stop living the lie. Start to slowly abandon out-of-reach purchases and begin to spend at your affordability level. Honor intangibles that you bring to the table, such as a sense of humor, integrity, perseverance, and so forth. Don't be like Haman, the insecure Persian official who needed the king's horse, the king's robe, and association with a noble prince to feel honored (ESTHER 6:7-9).

Frustration

Disappointment over thwarted plans or desires can send you running for the mall—especially when you have not embraced the truth that no man can thwart God's plans for your life. Listen up. If God wants your desires for a certain situation to come to pass, nobody can stop it. Perhaps He is working out in you something of more eternal value. Release it to Him. Father knows best.

The key to dealing with emotional spending is to acknowledge the emotion that is at work. The most critical question you will ask yourself is, "What is the best way to deal with this emotion?" Then you can address the issue of the item you are about to buy. Do I need it? Is it outside of my spending plan? Does it advance the ball down my financial court?

Ponder Your Purchases

She considers a field and buys it.

PROVERBS 31:16

"We'll take it!" we told the car salesman. When we left home that nice breezy morning, Darnell and I had no intention of returning with a brand-new red convertible. We had driven to a certain area to take a walk, and on the way home decided to stop by an auto dealership to indulge our curiosity. We had not even driven the car we would have traded in for this nice little upgrade. Several hours later, after the standard routine of the salesman checking with the manager in the back office a dozen times to get approval on the price, we drove off into the sunset. The next day, reality set in as we realized that we would need to sell our old car right away as well as pay for insurance on three vehicles. When all was said and done, the monthly cost of this car would be equal to the mortgage payment on an investment property in a good working-class neighborhood. We sold the car several months later and bought the property.

Impulsiveness is shunned in the Scriptures. "The

plans of the diligent lead to profit as surely as haste leads to poverty" (PROVERBS 21:5). This tendency towards hastiness is what leads us down the path to debt. We are the "now" generation, and in general we do not like delaying our gratification.

Many times God tries to protect us from our hasty decisions by throwing up red flags and putting up roadblocks all around us. But what do we often do? Put our heads in the sand and ignore them. Be careful if you are about to enter a transaction and things start falling apart.

My husband and I once invested in an ATM machine. (Yes, you read right—the kind that dispenses money!) The company's sales pitch was very enticing. The salesman, who claimed that he was a Christian, convinced us that investing in an ATM machine was the ideal way to make our money "work for us" with no effort on our part except to lease the machine for five years and own it at the end of that time. He promised—not in writing—(red flag...red flag...red flag!) that he would find the ideal location, put up appropriate signs, and the whole nine yards. After we signed the lease agreement, he came back and said that he had computed the payment incorrectly and that it would be an extra $50 per month (red flag...red flag...red flag!). Well, he reneged on all of his promises, and his company accepted no responsibility for them. He skipped town and left us with a noncancelable $426 monthly lease payment while the machine sat in our garage. We never found a profitable environment for it and ended up selling it at a substantial loss several years later.

How did we fall into this trap? First, we were too busy to pay attention to the details. Second, we assumed that the salesperson was sincere about his Christianity. We are now extremely cautious of investing in a deal solely because the promoter comes "in the name of Jesus." Finally, we didn't want to be like the wicked, lazy steward Jesus spoke of in Matthew 25 who buried the money he had been entrusted with rather than invest it. We really were trying to be good stewards. We wanted to maximize the return on our idle funds. We are much smarter today.

Now back to hastiness. When you recall the things you have bought on a whim, they were rarely items you needed. Rather, they represented temporary, emotion-filled desires. The Proverbs 31 woman *considered* her field before she bought it. Even if you are certain that something is a great idea, you should make it a habit of pondering your purchases.

Beware of hot deals and clearance sales. If you don't need an item and have no plans to use it, then it is not a deal no matter how low the price is. I have tons of stuff I have bought at a steal but have never worn. Impulsiveness makes you good bait for hungry salespeople, dishonest promoters, and other sales ploys. And speaking of salespeople, don't succumb to high-pressure deadlines. If it's meant for you to purchase an item, it will still be there the next day. Give yourself 24 hours to think about big-ticket purchases. Before you buy, ask yourself, "Is this a need or a desire?" "Can I afford it?" "Will I use it immediately?" "Do I already have something similar?" "How can I glorify God with this purchase?"

On a smaller scale of impulsiveness, I also challenge you to be on the alert when you are standing in line at the grocery store. Remember that the merchandise at the checkout counter is strategically positioned to encourage you to spend more money. You must prepare to resist the lure of sugar-laden snacks, gossip magazines, movies, and other impulse items.

You really can emulate Mrs. Proverbs 31 by considering your purchases. Heed the Holy Spirit's red light and don't run it. "In all thy ways acknowledge him, and he shall direct thy paths" (PROVERBS 3:6 KJV).

Day 22

End Your Enabling

We are each responsible for our own conduct.
GALATIANS 6:5 NLT

One of my brothers swears that he would be much further along financially if we had not spoiled him by enabling him to be irresponsible for such a long time. He's right. Because he was the youngest of seven children and my mother and father separated during his early years, I think we all wanted to make sure he didn't miss out on what life had to offer. Another one of my brothers became his surrogate father and bought him all kinds of expensive toys. He was often the envy of other neighborhood kids. As he grew older, he would borrow money from the family and face no consequences when he failed to pay us back. He even joined a Corvette car club and didn't own a Corvette—but I did. I spent a few weekend nights without transportation while he was cruising with the fellows. That was more than 30 years ago, and I had never heard of the word "enabler." I did not know that it was something undesirable.

Enabling negative behavior can have a severe impact

on your finances. Mothers are among the biggest enablers. Many of them seem to excuse the unacceptable behavior of their children—especially their adult sons. The scenario is the same in most families; only the names change. No matter how much the other siblings protest, Mom is steadily bailing the son out and declaring that she knows him better than anyone else—after all, they have a unique relationship.

Some grandparents are also enablers. I remember an 83-year-old widow coming to my office in tears because she had cosigned for a car loan for her grandson, who had defaulted on it. Further, she had obtained auto insurance for him, and he was involved in an accident where he was at fault. The victims sued her and prevailed. She was now being forced to sell her real estate to pay their claim. She was devastated. "I shouldn't have done it," she moaned.

Generally, it is a bad idea to cosign a loan for anybody, be it family members or friends. A person who needs a cosigner is obviously a high credit risk or the lender would not require the security of another person's credit. The Scriptures declare, "It is poor judgment to co-sign a friend's note, to become responsible for a neighbor's debts" (PROVERBS 17:18 NLT). This is not to say that you should not help your responsible son or daughter when they are in need. However, if you cannot afford to lose the money, think twice. Once you have been stung by somebody's default, wisdom will set in quickly.

When people enable their children, spouses, or anyone else to remain irresponsible by bailing them out or always being their safety net, they interrupt one of God's most effective teaching tools—sowing and then reaping the consequences of individual behavior. Real maturity occurs when people learn their lessons through experience. Enablers also hinder a person's spiritual and emotional development as well as jeopardize their own financial security. That's poor stewardship.

What about you? Let's see if you fit the profile of an enabler. Do you feel that you have a special relationship with an irresponsible person? Do you try to protect him from the criticism of others? Do you make most of the decisions for this person because you really think that you know what is best and must shield him from negative consequences? Do you perform any tasks for this person that he could learn to do for himself? Do you like feeling needed by this person?

Sometimes you can be so fearful of being rejected or alienated that you will enable your boomerang, able-bodied adult child to move back home with absolutely no financial responsibility. If your finances have been affected by your own enabling and you really don't have the heart to go cold turkey by saying it stops today, then start with a small thing to work your way out of the hole. Assign him a utility bill, then the phone bill, next a small amount for rent, have him buy his own food, or whatever will cause him to take some form of financial responsibility. This is real love. The Scriptures will back you up on this. "Even while we were with you, we gave you this rule: 'Whoever does not work should not eat'" (2 Thessalonians 3:10 NLT).

Ask God to give you the strength to say no to all requests from irresponsible people in your life—from family members who always need "a few dollars" to freeloading friends who never have their share of the bill when you eat out. Heed the apostle Paul's admonition, "Each one should carry his own load" (GALATIANS 6:5).

Day 23

Ditch Dishonesty

He thwarts the plans of the crafty, so that their
hands achieve no success.

JOB 5:12

Sometimes in the middle of a difficult financial situation, Satan convinces God's children that He is not going to come through for them. Some get anxious and conclude they'd better fix the situation the best way they can. At other times, the issue may not be one of adverse financial circumstances, but just the battle against plain old unadulterated greed. Whatever the motivation, in times like these, many will often make the unwise decision to abandon their integrity and succumb to dishonest measures.

When God's people resort to dishonesty, they are in effect saying to God, "I need or desire more money than I currently have, but I don't believe You will provide it. Therefore, I'll make my own way through ungodly means." This is a slap in God's face and results in very negative consequences.

Dishonesty can take several forms, including faking an injury in order to file a lawsuit, lying about your child's age, or using a wrong home address to get better auto insurance rates, to name a few.

One of the most powerful lessons on how to respond with integrity to an unfair employer is found in Genesis 29–31. It is the story of Jacob and his employer-uncle, Laban. Laban subjected Jacob to all kinds of deceit and inequities. He tricked Jacob into marrying his not-so-attractive older daughter, Leah, after he had agreed to work seven years for the younger, more attractive Rachel. Jacob was forced to work another seven years in order to marry the woman he loved. Laban changed Jacob's compensation agreement ten times. Notwithstanding, God blessed Jacob—who happened to be a tither—to succeed. He never lowered his standard of work in retaliation for Laban's unfair treatment. He later explained to his wives, "You know that I've worked for your father with all my strength, yet your father has cheated me by changing my wages ten times. However, God has not allowed him to harm me" (GENESIS 31:6-7).

God instructed Jacob to leave the unfair situation and to return to his homeland. He took his family and his hard-earned fortune and left without notice. When Laban heard about it, he gathered his posse and chased after him. However, before he could catch up with him, Laban had an encounter with God, who told him to be very careful with what he said to Jacob. When Laban overtook Jacob's party, Jacob confronted him with courage. "I have been with you for twenty years now.

Your sheep and goats have not miscarried, nor have I eaten rams from your flocks" (GENESIS 31:38).

If you find yourself in an unfair situation, resist the temptation to "eat rams" from your employer's flock. Don't make personal long-distance calls, take supplies home, or take extended lunches. Continue to perform as if God were evaluating your work and watching your every move—because He is. Continue to seek His favor regarding a raise or simply seek employment elsewhere. Remember that no one can disadvantage you when you walk uprightly with the Lord. Your divine destiny will prevail. "For the LORD Almighty has purposed, and who can thwart him? His hand is stretched out, and who can turn it back" (ISAIAH 14:27).

While God promises to open the windows of heaven and to pour out blessings to the tither, dishonesty will open the back door for them to flow out and never benefit you. Your blessings will end up in pockets with holes in them. I have heard of people who faked injuries and received large legal settlements, only to wonder later where all of the money went. "A fortune made by a lying tongue is a fleeting vapor and a deadly snare" (PROVERBS 21:6).

Know that dishonesty can impact your entire family. When God allowed the Israelites to defeat Jericho, He told them not to take any of the spoil. Notwithstanding, a young man named Achan took money and clothes and hid them in his tent. When his sin was discovered, he and his entire family were stoned and burned (JOSHUA 6–7).

Be careful not to set an example before your children

of lying and cheating for financial gain. They will more than likely copy your behavior and fall into the same pit. One of the best legacies one could leave for his family is one of integrity. "The righteous man walks in his integrity; his children are blessed after him" (PROVERBS 20:7 NKJV).

Riches unjustly gained can never really be enjoyed and have no positive end. As Christians, we are commanded to walk in integrity. Integrity is simply the act of integrating what we say we believe and what we actually do. Yes, even professing Christians can have an integrity problem. When we fail in this area, others see it as a disconnection in our testimony. Many unsaved folks are turned off by such hypocrisy.

During this 30-day commitment to start taming your finances, search yourself and determine if there are any areas of your life where you may not be walking in integrity. Integrity also includes keeping your word. When people cannot depend on you to repay your loans or to show up when promised, they will not be inclined to extend any loans or bail out measures to you when you may need it most. Do not rationalize your behavior. Simply take whatever steps are necessary to slam shut this back door.

I have asked God to trouble my conscience so that I can't sleep, function, or proceed in any endeavor where I am not operating in complete integrity. Would you be willing to pray such a prayer?

Day 24

Watch Wastefulness

"Now gather the leftovers," Jesus told his disciples,
"so that nothing is wasted."

JOHN 6:12 NLT

Jesus set a great example for frugality. Even though
He had performed a miracle and fed a crowd of 5,000
men and an undisclosed number of women and children with only five loaves and two small fishes, He
instructed His disciples to gather up the leftovers. When
it was all said and done, they had gathered 12 basket-
fuls. *Now, Jesus,* you may wonder, *was that necessary?*
You could have thrown that extra bread away. All you
had to do was perform another miracle and make more
bread when You needed it. Through His actions, Jesus
was showing the importance of not squandering what
God has provided—even when it appears that you do
not need the excess.

I talked to a couple recently who had lived a rather
lavish lifestyle, but through a series of misfortunes had
lost everything. They are starting to rebuild their lives

and are working at jobs that pay much less than what they were used to making. I queried them about the role they had played in their financial decline, and they confessed that they were partly responsible. I concluded from a casual observation of their current behavior that a lot of their old wasteful habits were still alive and well. They called it "generosity" when they gave a 95 percent tip to the restaurant's parking attendant. By no means am I opposed to such bigheartedness, but when you are trying to stabilize your finances, you need to understand that frugality is a significant part of spirituality and that God is not pleased when we engage in extravagance.

In one of His parables, Jesus talked about a son who convinced his father to give him his inheritance before the appointed time. "A few days later this younger son packed all his belongings and took a trip to a distant land, and there he wasted all his money on wild living" (LUKE 15:13 NLT). When the economy turned sour, he could only find work feeding a farmer's swine. He almost starved to death. At one point, he became so hungry that he had to eat the pods that the farmer fed to the swine. I can imagine him sitting there by the trough dividing the food between himself and the pigs: "swine," "mine," "swine," "mine." He then realized that his father's servants were living better than this. He humbled himself and headed home. His merciful father was glad to receive him and gave him a big welcome back party. Of course, by having the party, the father was by no means condoning his son's wastefulness, but rather celebrating his coming to his senses.

Are you wasteful in any area of your life, or do you

actively seek ways to practice frugality? For instance, do you allow your children to open a can of soda, take a few sips, and then trash it? Did you know that there are special lids available at the supermarket that will allow you to seal the can and preserve the fizz? Are you too embarrassed to ask for a doggie bag when you eat out? Do you bring home leftovers from your restaurant dining and then allow them to spoil in the refrigerator before you can consume them? Do you consider reusing plastic lunch bags, especially when you only use them for dry goods such as chips and cookies? They can be recycled at least once after a quick swipe with a damp towel. Do you always turn the lights off when you leave the room? Do you use both sides of the paper when printing drafts of reports—at home and at work?

I have practiced frugality as far back as I can remember. In fact, Darnell teases that I squeeze each dollar so tightly it's a wonder I don't rub George Washington's face right off the front of it. Yes, I turn the bottle upside down and get the last drop out of everything. I pick up every penny I find when I'm out walking. As Benjamin Franklin said, "A penny saved is a penny earned." I use vinegar and water instead of the fancy cleaners to clean glass and shiny surfaces. I do everything I can to save money—not to hoard it, but so that I can share it. I can't think of a single thing I have ever purchased that has brought more joy than writing a check to someone who desperately needs it. We are never more like Christ than when we are giving.

I want to be careful to balance our discussion by

warning that we should not allow our desire to be frugal to keep us from fully enjoying the things that are within the bounds of what God allows. I thoroughly enjoy the breathtaking view of the city from my home. My husband and I have made great sacrifices in putting the needs of God's house before our own desires. Therefore, we refuse to allow Satan to make us feel guilty about what God has provided.

Frugality is not a call to poverty, and it certainly should not take the fun out of our lives. It is important that we enjoy the abundant life that Christ came to give us. It is equally important to understand that abundance is not to be equated with extravagance. God blesses His children with abundance so that they can bless others with their overflow. If we are all poverty-stricken, how will we have an overflow?

Frugality is simply avoiding waste. Wastefulness will keep your finances in a tailspin. Frugality is evidence that God can trust you with increased resources because you have learned how to manage what He has already supplied.

Day 25

Improve Your Image

Man looks at the outward appearance.

1 SAMUEL 16:7

After King Nebuchadnezzar of Babylon had besieged and conquered Jerusalem, he decided to train a select group of the young captives from the royal families for palace service in Babylon. He had some very strict criteria for them to meet:

> *"Select only strong, healthy, and good-looking young men," he said. "Make sure they are well versed in every branch of learning, are gifted with knowledge and good sense, and have the poise needed to serve in the royal palace. Teach these young men the language and literature of the Babylonians"* (DANIEL 1:4 NLT).

Are you qualified to serve in the king's house? Do you give the appearance of being healthy and energetic? Don't be in denial here. Look in the mirror and be honest. If you were an employer evaluating you, would you perceive yourself as a great candidate? How good is your grammar and diction? If necessary, you may want to take classes and learn to articulate well—especially if you have a thick accent. It is important that you be able to communicate effectively. Have you invested in yourself by taking classes or buying books to polish your image? If so, potential employers or clients may assume that you obviously require more income than the average interviewee. They may conclude that offering you less money would not be appropriate.

Be careful with your image when one of your company's top executives or a key client is picking up the lunch tab. You don't want to appear to be starving or too unsophisticated. Skip the doggie bag. I asked a staff person to join a banking executive and me for lunch. Because he had already had a substantial amount of food on his break, he was not really hungry. Rather than order an appetizer or other light fare, he kept bemoaning the fact that he wasn't hungry. Finally noticing the server's impatience to take his order, he said, "I'll have a turkey burger to go." I was horrified. I gave him a killer look and he ordered shrimp cocktail.

When you know the rules of etiquette and other social skills, you can be confident in any setting. Remember that confidence is rooted in knowledge—so learn all that you can. The local library, bookstores, and the Internet are great sources for image-polishing, confidence-building information.

Make sure that you dress appropriately—even on your company's casual occasions. I am so turned off by employees who have no idea of what "casual day" means. Although it is a time to ditch suits, ties, and hosiery, some people go to the extreme and dress as though they were going to the beach or about to do spring cleaning. Despite the fact that most companies have written guidelines for such days, I have seen men show up in baggy sweatpants, while female employees sport cutoffs or outfits with splits up to the unspeakable and inappropriate cleavage. The workplace really isn't the place to be sexy—unless that's how you plan to get ahead. Of course, Christians know that if they do their jobs well, God is in charge of their promotions.

Also, have a basic wardrobe that can fit all occasions. For men, at least one dark suit is a must. I know a guy in middle management who received a last-minute invitation to represent his company at a black-tie event with other senior executives. When I asked him what he planned to wear, he stated that he only had a shirt and tie and did not own a single jacket. I told him to borrow one because without it, he was going to stick out like a sore thumb. For women, a simple black dress and some look-like-the-real-thing pearls will carry the day.

I know that Scripture says, "Man looks at the outward appearance, but the LORD looks at the heart" (1 SAMUEL 16:7). In my seminars, I teach that these are two independent thoughts. When dealing with man, you would be wise to focus on your outward appearance; when dealing with God, make sure that the intentions of your heart are pure. Enough said.

I know a woman who went to work for a Fortune 500 company and was quite concerned when she, as a new hire, was given preferential treatment over a gentleman who had been with the company for many years and had much more experience than she. When she questioned a member of upper management about this, he replied, "Oh, you are much more sophisticated than he." Now mind you, sophistication does not mean that she ate with a raised pinky or that she affected a certain aristocratic air. That is a turnoff to everybody. She simply demonstrated more refined behavior than this other employee. He was known for his unusual and very loud laughter—which could be heard all over the floor where he worked—and somehow he seemed to find everything funny. To boot, he was the source of much company gossip. His behavior had a definite impact on his finances. It cost him promotions and respect from upper management.

Even though I have focused on employees in this discussion, these principles apply to anyone who interacts with others who can impact their finances. Even if you are an entrepreneur, your appearance and professionalism will not go unnoticed by your customers.

Let's not tiptoe around this issue of a polished image. We should not pooh-pooh it as some straight-laced, old-fashioned thinking. Believe me, the image you present to the world matters.

Put Off Procrastination

If you wait for perfect conditions,
you will never get anything done.

ECCLESIASTES 11:4 NLT

"Never put off until tomorrow what you can do today." It sounds trite now, but this admonishment from our teachers or parents was some of the best advice anyone could give us. Life is too short to get stuck in analysis paralysis. Dr. Myles Munroe says that the graveyard is one of the richest places on the earth because lots of ideas and dreams are buried there. Is procrastination robbing you of your dreams and financial goals?

Let's look at some of the root causes of procrastination and understand what we must do from a practical sense to overcome it.

Fear of Failure

Many people feel inadequate to perform necessary tasks and dread being a big flop. Is this true of you? Well, you may not find these words inspiring, but you are indeed inadequate—apart from God. Accept the fact that without Him you can do nothing, but with Him you can do all things. Also understand that failure is not fatal. It just may be part of God's strategy to fine-tune your skills, strengthen your faith, and develop your humility so that you can be very clear on who gets the credit for your ultimate success. God never gives anybody a responsibility without giving him the ability to respond.

Fear of Success

There is indeed a downside to becoming a financial success. There is the possibility you will be alienated or rejected by your low-achieving, unambitious buddies, family members, or other acquaintances. Now, some will genuinely support you, but others may view your success as a reminder of what they could have become. Also, people tend to raise their expectations of successful people. Thus, you may feel you can no longer be your old, junk-food-eating, no-makeup-wearing self. I know a woman who has dealt with this fear. She always dreaded that great success would put her out of touch with the regular folks whom she loved and with whom she wanted to hang out. She feared that she would be doomed to loneliness because people would assume that she was beyond their reach.

And what about those who develop a need for your funds to bail them out? Do you fear being hated or rejected for saying no to them because of their financial irresponsibility? Finally, what if you cannot maintain the success? Just the thought of losing it all can create a high level of anxiety.

Are you willing to allow these possibilities to doom you to a life sentence in "mediocrity prison" where you have just enough money to survive and can never be a blessing to anybody? God forbid! He will give you the grace to deal with whatever challenges that arise. You cannot figure out your life from start to finish and then try to fit all the pieces neatly into the puzzle. There is not even a picture of the finished product on the box called life. Our daily walk is one of faith. "We walk by faith, not by sight" (2 CORINTHIANS 5:7 NKJV).

Shortsightedness

Some people procrastinate to avoid the inconvenience, the personal sacrifice, or other short-term unpleasantness associated with achieving their goal. They have allowed these things to overshadow future benefit. For example, suppose that you have delayed in furthering your education. Perhaps you have rationalized, "I would love to go back to school, but it'll take me two years to finish the program. I'll be 40 in two years. It's too late now. Besides, I'd have to give up my weekends to study." Well, guess what? You'll be 40 in two years whether you go back to school or not. As for the weekends, finishing your program is not an eternal project. Time will surely fly. Quit looking for excuses not to proceed. Just how important is your dream to you? If Jesus had been shortsighted, none of us would have received salvation. Instead, He "was willing to die a shameful death on the

cross because of the joy he knew would be his afterward"
(HEBREWS 12:2 NLT).

If you have been procrastinating about something,
set aside some time to pray alone and with a friend to
find out if God is indeed leading you to pursue the con-
templated goal or if it's just an idea that emanated from
your own fleshly desire—or someone else's prompting.
Once you are convinced that it is a God idea rather than
just a good idea, ask Him to start opening doors for the
idea to come to fruition. Of course, you will need to step
through them as He opens them.

How many times have you had an original idea,
only to sit on it and later hear that someone else had
put it into action? Oh, the self-kicking that takes place.
"I shoulda, coulda, woulda…" I have to admit that I am
the complete opposite of a procrastinator. I tend to want
to do everything the moment I think of it. When I saw
the need for a "confident dining" etiquette card, I called
a printer on Monday who informed me that he did not
do projects requiring graphic arts work. "However," he
said, "I have a friend who does, and he just happens to
be here now." "Please put him on the phone," I replied.
I faxed him my rendition of the card and was selling
them by Friday. I have made a few revisions since, but
the point is that I got started. Everything does not have
to be perfect the first time around.

What idea are you sitting on today? What practical
steps can you take in the next three days that would put
you on the path to bringing the idea to fruition?

Day 27

Profit from Your Passion

She makes linen garments and sells them,
and supplies the merchants with sashes.

PROVERBS 31:24

The Proverbs 31 woman is at it again. We see in Proverbs 31:22 that she has a passion for sewing, for she "makes coverings for her bed; she is clothed in fine linen and purple." At first it appears that this is just a hobby or a fun pastime, but in verse 24 we see her profiting from her craft. "She makes linen garments and sells them."

God has given every person a gift that has value to someone else. The apostle Paul declared, "I wish that all men were as I am. But each man has his own gift from God; one has this gift, another has that" (1 CORINTHIANS 7:7). Perhaps you have convinced yourself that you have no gift to be passionate about. If so, think again. What do you do really well? What have others told you that you do well? If success were guaranteed, and if there was no potential for embarrassment or financial loss, what would you be doing at this point in your life? What fear is holding you back? Do you know anyone else who is doing what you'd like to do? No one? Then consider that you may be called to be a trailblazer!

Most studies show that the vast majority of people are not satisfied with their jobs. What makes many dissatisfied is their assumption that they have no other immediate options. Others are not willing to invest the time, energy, and funds to learn additional skills or to venture out in their own business endeavor. I challenge you to bring your passion to your work environment. You do not have to be self-employed in order to love what you do. I have held a few positions in which I could hardly wait to get to the job to pursue my passion of implementing effective processes, negotiating difficult agreements, and solving whatever problems would arise. Problem solving is one of my passions. When others run away from an issue as if escaping from a burning house, I can be found with the water hose running toward it.

Your passion will not go unnoticed in any environment and can indeed result in financial gain. Of course, on a job you may not have the freedom to pursue your passion to the fullest extent, but if you maximize your experience there, it could very well be the springboard to realizing your ultimate dream. Whether on the job or self-employed, Scripture admonishes us to be enthusiastic no matter what we do. "Whatever your hand finds to do, do it with all your might, for in the grave, where you are going, there is neither working nor planning nor knowledge nor wisdom" (ECCLESIASTES 9:10).

Watch out for folks who try to put out your fire. Saboteurs of your passion are a dime a dozen. Some people simply may not share your passion for your area of interest, while others are just plain envious because your efforts remind them of what they could be doing. You have to treat such people as you would a toxic substance—minimize your exposure to them.

To balance our discussion, please understand that your desire to profit from your passion is not a license to be consumed by it, burning the midnight oil, and never smelling the roses. I used to jokingly say I had two speeds: fast and off. I was always pursuing my next goal with a vengeance. My strength of being focused had become a liability. Life is not to be lived at extremes.

Finally, you may have to *plant* before you *profit*. I have delivered many speeches for free or for "love tokens" that ranged from gift baskets to outdated jewelry. I have planted seeds I wish to sow. Further, for me the message was and still is more important than the money. Oddly enough, though, teaching the message through books, tapes, CDs, speaking engagements, and other avenues has evolved into a profitable endeavor.

So what about you? What are some gifts you could put to work right now with passion? Baking? Gardening? Sewing? Car detailing? Editing? It's time to get going. The money will follow your passion.

Day 28

Face the Facts with Faith

Without weakening in his faith, [Abraham]
faced the fact that his body was as good as dead—
since he was about a hundred years old—and
that Sarah's womb was also dead.

ROMANS 4:19-20

The story of Abraham inspires me. He had the unique ability to face facts but not allow them to weaken his faith. The man was 100 years old with a 90-year-old wife well past childbearing age, yet he believed they would still have their own son—and they did.

Have you ever run into a situation in which all the facts were stacked against you? Several years ago when my husband and I decided to "move up" from our first home, the price of the house we had set our hearts on was out of our predetermined range. Our goal for wanting to move was to be closer to our church so that we could serve the ministry more effectively. We were growing weary of the commute. I had long desired to have a home with a view of the Los Angeles skyline. What a sight that is with beautiful mountain ranges set as a backdrop. It just so happened that the church was only minutes away from a very hilly neighborhood with awesome views. Our pastor, the late Dr. H. Marvin Smith, told us not to limit God to our budget on this transaction because we had been faithful in our service and our stewardship. We found a house we fell in love with and made an offer on it. The seller immediately rejected it. We did not feel led to increase the offer, so we said, "The will of the Lord be done." A few weeks later, the seller relented but demanded a 10 percent deposit within a few days. We had one percent on hand. God strategically had my very unsupportive, immediate boss leave town during this period. I worked for a Fortune 500 company at the time and had favor with the corporate treasurer's administrative assistant. When I appealed to him directly for a temporary loan until we could sell our existing home, he approved it immediately—without a set due date or collateral. This was nothing short of a miracle. After overcoming numerous other roadblocks that threatened to derail the purchase, we finally moved into the house and enjoyed many years of rich fellowship with our church members, family, and friends. It was truly God's house.

I can recount an endless number of other situations where it looked as though the facts would thwart my financial blessings. I even went to graduate school on a fellowship and earned a masters' degree in business finance from the University of Southern California—after being told that I was rejected due to the low score I had made on the entrance exam. The fact was that they only accepted candidates who scored at least a minimum number of points. I told the Lord, "You're going to look really bad because I have been confessing for the past six months that I was going on a leave of absence from my job to go back to school." I was so disappointed that I went to Europe and spent the money I had saved in anticipation of being accepted. However, God was working behind the scenes. One month before school was to start, they informed me they had changed their minds and would be granting me the all-expense-paid-plus-a-stipend fellowship. I didn't know whether to cry or shout. I was so financially motivated that I finished the two-year program in seven months!

We must never allow facts to overshadow our faith. The Bible is filled with stories of faith overriding facts. For example, Peter, James, and John were calling it a day after fishing all night with no success when Jesus came along and instructed them to try again. Now, if the fish were not biting at night, surely the daytime was the worst time to expect any results. Nevertheless, they ignored these facts, acted on Jesus' word, and experienced a miraculous, net-breaking catch (LUKE 5).

Have you allowed certain facts to dash your financial hopes? Does your FICO score place you among the "undesirables"? Is your debt ratio outside of your bank's traditional lending range? No down payment? No collateral? Not enough time on the job? No credit history at all? Is there a desperately needed item outside your budget? Are you going to succumb to these facts, or do you have the faith to ask God for a miracle? Know that just as people major in certain subjects in college, God has a major also. He majors in impossibilities.

Now I'd like to give a word of advice. It is a lot easier to exercise faith when you have been obedient. Long before Abraham received the son he was promised, he had a history of obeying God. When God got ready to bless him abundantly, he told Abraham to leave his pagan-worshipping relatives and to relocate to some not-yet-determined place that God would show him. There is no evidence that Abraham even hesitated (see Genesis 12). He obeyed immediately. He responded in a similar manner when God told him to offer Isaac, his long-awaited son of promise, as a sacrifice. He obeyed without question, and God found a substitute for the sacrificial offering (GENESIS 22). What a model of faith!

Each time I have needed divine intervention in a financial transaction, I have been quick to remind God of His promises to the faithful. Because faith comes by hearing, I memorize His promises. I write them on the back of old business cards to recite when walking. I put them in picture frames to keep in view during the day. I type them in large fonts and post them on my treadmill. I decree them out loud. "Thou shalt also decree a thing, and it shall be established unto thee: and the light shall shine upon thy ways" (JOB 22:28 KJV). This builds my faith and takes the teeth out of the facts. I try to keep in mind that faith "is the confident assurance that what we hope for is going to happen. It is the evidence of things we cannot yet see" (HEBREWS 11:1-2 NLT). In the words of my friend Dr. Judy McAllister, "The more faith you have, the less evidence you need."

What facts are you facing today? Decree the Word of God and don't let them overshadow your faith.

Day 29

Seek Support

Plans go wrong for lack of advice;
many counselors bring success.

PROVERBS 15:22 NLT

No man is an island. While you may indeed feel isolated in your attempt to tame your finances, God does not expect you to try to solve your problems alone. From friends to formal debt counseling agencies, help is only a call away.

The first place to seek help when your finances are out of control is from a trusted, financially astute, Bible-believing friend or family member who can give you caring support, good advice, and help you to stay accountable. "Carry each other's burdens, and in this way you will fulfill the law of Christ" (GALATIANS 6:2). Notwithstanding, I find that most people are too embarrassed for someone to know about the bad judgment they have exercised that got them to where they are. This kind of thinking will keep you in the red. Ask the Holy Spirit to help you get beyond the shame so that you can quickly make your escape from financial bondage. Further, if it is of any comfort, there are tons of people in your same situation.

A few years ago I sat down with a very close relative who was in dire financial straits. We spent hours poring over credit card bills, payroll check stubs, and other documents. She had gone through a divorce and her husband had been quite irresponsible in handling his finances. A car repossession, various delinquency charges, and a few other financial dings painted a bleak picture for her future credit. Further, to ease the emotional impact of the divorce and to get back into the swing of things, she had resorted to "mall therapy" and ran up quite a few credit card bills. While I was indeed sympathetic to her plight, even to the point of wanting to bail her out by consolidating all of her consumer debt into a personal loan, I decided she needed the discipline of digging her way out of the hole. I cringed even more when I saw that she hardly gave anything to her church. Although I didn't see a way that she could do it, I still suggested that she begin to give God His due. We worked out a strategic plan that she committed to following. I made a few follow-up accountability calls over the next few months. Three years later, she now pays her tithes and is on stable financial footing. She also purchased a home and has been promoted several times on her job. We never discussed the details of her situation with other family members.

If you do not have a relative or friend who can provide significant guidance and accountability, and you really don't have a clue as to what to do, you may want to try the services of a credit counseling agency. Over nine million debt-challenged Americans seek help from credit counseling agencies annually. In recent years, some agencies have received a bad reputation for pressuring clients to pay high "voluntary" fees and for quickly putting them into debt-management plans that require high fees. There have been a few horror stories of debt-management firms collecting clients' monthly bill funds and not sending payments in to the creditors on a timely basis. Therefore, it would be wise to make every effort to find a reputable Christian agency whose advice is based upon biblical principles and that takes time to understand your particular circumstances. Be sure that the agency puts in writing the fees that will be charged and that you understand and can afford them. Absent a personal referral, do an Internet search to find one in your area. Stay away from secular agencies that may encourage you to put your obligation to God on the back burner until it makes more sense on paper. You are going to need favor and supernatural intervention to get your finances back on track. Giving shows that you are exercising your faith and planting seeds for the power of God to work in your life. "But my righteous one will live by faith. And if he shrinks back, I will not be pleased with him" (HEBREWS 10:38).

Here's the bottom line on what you can expect in general from a credit counseling agency: They will charge you a setup fee and a monthly maintenance fee for their services. They will contact your creditors to work out lower payments, request a stop to late fees and other penalties, and even work out a reduction or elimination of interest charges. They do not contact utilities, insurance companies, or secured creditors (those who hold a security interest in the things that you have purchased, such as your home, cars, etc.). If this is the kind of help that you need to get out of the red, go for it. "Listen to advice and accept instruction, and in the end you will be wise" (PROVERBS 19:20).

If the thought of potential credit counseling fraud scares you away, you may decide to go solo in working your way out of the pit. Do not despair. You know what to do. Go back and read the previous chapters. Develop a plan and work it. Be patient. It took more than a month to get where you are, and it will take more than a month to get out of the red. It really is like dieting. Just be consistent in applying the principles we have discussed. Listen to the prompting of the Holy Spirit. When He flashes the red light, heed it. "You guide me with your counsel, and afterward you will take me into glory" (PSALM 73:24).

Day 30

Cultivate Contentment

Not that I speak in regard to need,
for I have learned in whatever
state I am, to be content.

PHILIPPIANS 4:11 NKJV

Someone once said, "The trouble with most people is their earning capacity doesn't match their yearning capacity." So when is enough, enough? Do you find yourself unable to enjoy what you do have because your thoughts always seem to wander to what you don't have? Contentment should be the goal of every person who desires to walk in financial freedom. In our "more, more, more" society, anyone who is content is viewed by the stressed-out masses as lazy and unambitious. It is interesting to note that various surveys show that people felt richer in the '50s than they do now when we have bigger houses, DVD players, low-calorie frozen dinners, cable TV, cell phones, and the Internet. Why is this so? I'd say that it is because we are overwhelmed with trying to obtain and maintain too much stuff. Most people have not learned how to be content. Benjamin Franklin captured our dilemma with his memorable words, "Money never made a man happy yet, nor will it. There is nothing in its nature to produce happiness. The more a man has, the more he wants. Instead of filling a vacuum, it makes one."

Let's look at contentment as taught in the Bible. Paul said that "godliness with contentment is great gain" (1 TIMOTHY 6:6 KJV). We must understand that discontentment is a state of the mind in which one never quite feels satisfied with his present possessions. On the other hand, contentment is a state of the heart. A contented Christian says, "Father, I thank You for everything I am blessed to have right now, and I rest in Your promise to give me the desires of my heart and to meet every need I have according to Your riches in glory. You see the financial goals I have submitted to You. I receive Your grace to do all that I am supposed to do, and I leave the rest to You." You will gain joy and satisfaction once you decide that enough is enough.

To be content does not mean to be complacent. A complacent person is satisfied with his circumstances and desires no more. A Christian who is content is satisfied that his material blessings are on a planned delivery schedule and at the appointed time will come into reality. We must understand that God has always worked on a set timetable. He sent His Son to the earth in "the fullness of time" (GALATIANS 4:4 NKJV). He promises to exalt us in "due time" (1 PETER 5:6). Your financial blessing will come at the appointed time. You must stay surrendered to God's sovereign schedule. Oh, what a relief it is to relax in the assurance that the blessing is for a set time. It is no wonder, then, that the apostle Paul exclaimed that godliness with contentment is great gain (1 TIMOTHY 6:6). One who has achieved this level of spiritual maturity has indeed gained the victory over anxiety and the gravitational pull of materialism.

Let's look at a couple of antidotes for discontentment.

Gratitude

One of the key steps to slaying discontentment is to become grateful for everything. Take nothing for granted. At the end of each day, take a few minutes to remind yourself of every provision God has made for you and your family that day. Did you drive a car to work today? Did you have a choice of what outfit to wear today? Were you able to obtain the food you wanted today?

Solid Relationships

A key factor in avoiding the pitfall of discontentment is to become more relationship focused and less "stuff" conscious. When we read the account of the Shunammite woman to whom Elisha wanted to express his appreciation for adding a room onto her home solely for him and his servant, we immediately sense her contentment:

> He said to his servant Gehazi, "Call the Shunammite." So he called her, and she stood before him. Elisha said to him,

*"Tell her, 'you have gone to all this trouble
for us. Now what can be done for you?
Can we speak on your behalf to the king or
the commander of the army?'" She replied,
"I have a home among my own people"*
(2 KINGS 4:12-13).

Even though she was barren, she had not focused
on what was missing in her life, but rather on what she
had—meaningful relationships. She was not concerned
with climbing the social ladder. She had no need for
anyone to speak to the king on her behalf, thank you.
She had found contentment in her relationships. Many
people will spend thousands of dollars to go to faraway
places and interact with strangers whom they will never
see again rather than investing quality time in building
meaningful relationships at home.

The Shunammite woman had the wisdom to say,
"I have enough." While she was blessed with enough
abundance to be able to build a room addition for the
prophet, nothing suggests that she was in pursuit of
more. She was content to serve God and to honor Him
with the resources with which she had been blessed.

I know a couple that has made a very deliberate
and wise decision to pursue a simpler lifestyle in order
to spend more time with their family. I am certain they
would like more material possessions, but they have
chosen to avoid the stress associated with trying to
acquire and pay for more, more, and more. They have
said, "We have enough." Consequently, they are much
more creative in their social activities, and there is an

aura of peace that surrounds them. Their more stressed-out peers seek their company as a haven from the never-enough-stuff madness that permeates our current society. Jesus gave a strong warning to His disciples, and it is still appropriate: "Beware! Don't be greedy for what you don't have. Real life is not measured by how much we own" (LUKE 12:15 NLT).

The ability to be content is a spiritual discipline that will probably be a lifelong quest for most of us as we seek to tame our finances. The key is to get started today.

Epilogue

You may not have been able to put into practice every suggestion in this book in 30 days, but you can make a commitment to *begin* implementing the principles that will lead you from bondage to financial freedom. Managing your money effectively is about making right choices. The most important choice is to make God your partner in every transaction and to let Him have the last say. Study the Scriptures on money and stewardship so that you get a good feel for God's views and directives regarding your finances.

Practice understanding your own motives and inner needs when planning your expenditures; sometimes they are not always crystal clear. There may be times when they are evident, but you may not want to face the truth. You will find freedom and peace when you let the light of God's Word challenge the things that are contrary to His best for your finances. "But you desire honesty from the heart, so you can teach me to be wise in my inmost being" (PSALM 51:6 NLT).

Do not make the mistake of planning to put God

on hold until you are on an even keel. You may never get there without Him. He wants to guide you to your victory, for He "is able to do immeasurably more than all we ask or imagine, according to his power that is at work within us" (EPHESIANS 3:20).

Stop, think, and pray before you pay.

Appendix A

What I Own and What I Owe

Assets (What I Own):

Cash in Banks   _____

Stocks and Bonds   _____

Cash Value of Whole-Life
   Insurance Policy   _____

Jewelry/Art/Clothing   _____

Vehicles   _____

House/Condo   _____

Rental Property   _____

Other: _____   _____

Other: _____   _____

Total Assets   ===============

Liabilities (What I Owe):

Credit Card #1: _____   _____

Credit Card #2: _____   _____

Credit Card #3: _____   _____

Auto Loan   _____

Mortgage Loan   _____

School Loan   _____

Other: _____   _____

Other: _____   _____

Total Liabilities   ===============

Net Worth (Assets Minus Liabilities)   ===============

Appendix B

What I Make and Where It Goes

Take-Home Income (After Taxes):

Source 1: _____

Source 2: _____

Total Income _____

Less: Tithes/Offerings _____

Less: Savings _____

Net Cash Available _____

Fixed Expenses:

Rent/Mortgage _____

Auto Loan/Bus Fare _____

Auto Insurance _____

Credit Card Payment: _____

Credit Card Payment: _____

Water/Gas _____

Electricity _____

Medical/Life Insurance _____

Total Fixed Expenses _____

Variable Expenses:

Auto Repairs/Maintenance _____

Lunches _____

Groceries _____

Recreation/Cable TV _____

Laundry/Dry Cleaning _____

Telephone _____

Gasoline _____

Clothing _____

Grooming (Hair/Nails/Etc.) _____

Vacation Reserve _____

Other: _____

Other: _____

Total Variable Expenses ==========

Total All Expenses: ==========

Net Excess (Deficit) Cash ==========

Appendix C

Tracking Your Variable Expenditures

Week 1	Mon	Tue	Wed
Gasoline			
Auto Repair			
Car Wash			
Snacks/Coffee (AM)			
Snacks/Coffee (PM)			
Lunch			
Dinner Out			
Groceries			
Recreation			
Manicure/Pedicure			
Cell Phone			
Telephone			
Gasoline			
Clothing			
Dry Cleaning			
Hair			
Cosmetics / Toiletries			
Other:			
Other:			
Other:			
Other:			
Other:			
Total Expenditures			

Thu	Fri	Sat	Sun

Week 2	Mon	Tue	Wed
Gasoline			
Auto Repair			
Car Wash			
Snacks/Coffee (AM)			
Snacks/Coffee (PM)			
Lunch			
Dinner Out			
Groceries			
Recreation			
Manicure/Pedicure			
Cell Phone			
Telephone			
Gasoline			
Clothing			
Dry Cleaning			
Hair			
Cosmetics / Toiletries			
Other:			
Other:			
Other:			
Other:			
Other:			
Total Expenditures			

Thu	Fri	Sat	Sun

Week 3	Mon	Tue	Wed
Gasoline			
Auto Repair			
Car Wash			
Snacks/Coffee (AM)			
Snacks/Coffee (PM)			
Lunch			
Dinner Out			
Groceries			
Recreation			
Manicure/Pedicure			
Cell Phone			
Telephone			
Gasoline			
Clothing			
Dry Cleaning			
Hair			
Cosmetics / Toiletries			
Other:			
Other:			
Other:			
Other:			
Other:			
Total Expenditures			

Thu	Fri	Sat	Sun

Week 4	Mon	Tue	Wed
Gasoline			
Auto Repair			
Car Wash			
Snacks/Coffee (AM)			
Snacks/Coffee (PM)			
Lunch			
Dinner Out			
Groceries			
Recreation			
Manicure/Pedicure			
Cell Phone			
Telephone			
Gasoline			
Clothing			
Dry Cleaning			
Hair			
Cosmetics / Toiletries			
Other:			
Other:			
Other:			
Other:			
Other:			
Total Expenditures			

Thu	Fri	Sat	Sun

Appendix D

*Premarital 20/20 Vision Quiz
for Financial Compatibility* ©

Instructions: The purpose of this exam is to determine if a couple has the same vision for their finances. Each party must honestly answer "T" for true or "F" for false to each of the questions below. When finished, they should compare their answers and candidly discuss areas for potential conflict. A "true" answer to any of the questions by either party should be considered a red flag that should not be ignored.

	Him	Her	
1.	____	____	I do not believe in or practice tithing to the church.
2.	____	____	I do not systematically save money out of my income.
3.	____	____	I have less than four weeks' take-home pay in the bank.
4.	____	____	I do not maintain a checking account. I prefer to pay my bills by cash or money order.
5.	____	____	I have no dream of purchasing a home.
6.	____	____	I buy status symbols (cars, clothes, etc) that fit the image I wish to portray to others.

7. ____ ____ I do not believe a wife should work.

8. ____ ____ I believe whoever makes the most money should have the final say on household financial matters.

9. ____ ____ I believe all bills should be split 50-50.

10. ____ ____ I feel there is nothing wrong with a spouse having a "secret" bank account as long as s/he pays her/his share of the bills.

11. ____ ____ I do not participate in my employer's matching contribution retirement program, or, if self-employed, I do not make contributions toward my retirement.

12. ____ ____ I have had at least three different employers in the past five years.

13. ____ ____ I often pick up the tab when I eat out with family and friends—even if I have to charge the bill because I am short on cash.

14. ____ ____ My FICO score is under 675.

15. ____ ____ I see no problem in cosigning for or extending a personal loan to a close friend or family member.

16. ____ ____ I am only able to pay the minimum payment on my credit card and other consumer debt.

17. ____ ____ I am currently delinquent on a personal loan or other debt.

18. ____ ____ I have filed bankruptcy in the past ten years.

19. ____ ____ I have a financial commitment to my former wife, parent, child, failed business, or _____ that will continue after I am married.

20. ____ ____ I feel it is okay to tell a "little white lie" to save money or to gain other financial advantage.

Appendix E

The Credit Card Trap

The chart below shows that a $5,000 credit card purchase would cost $12,115 if paid off using only the minimum required monthly payment. It would take 26 years to reduce the balance to zero. The outstanding balance and the minimum payment at the end of various points in time are shown to demonstrate how the system works to stretch out the debt.

Assumption: Pay only the Minimum Required amount each month of 2.5% of the outstanding balance. Interest rate: 18% annually, or 1.5% Per Month

Month #	Year #	Min. Pymnt.	Interest	Bal. Reduction	Remain. Bal.
					5,000.00
1	0.1	125.00	75.00	50.00	4,950.00
2	0.2	123.75	74.25	49.50	4,900.50
12	1.0	111.92	67.15	44.77	4,431.92
24	2.0	99.20	59.52	39.68	3,928.39
60	5.0	69.09	41.45	27.63	2,735.78
120	10.0	37.80	22.68	15.12	1,496.90
180	15.0	20.68	12.41	8.27	819.04
240	20.0	11.32	6.79	4.53	448.14
313	26.1	8.50	0.13	8.37	-

Total Paid 12,115.43 7,115.42   5,000.00

If the original minimum payment of $125 had been sent in each month, the balance would have been repaid in 62 months or 5.2 years versus 26.1 years.

How to Contact the Author

Deborah Smith Pegues is an experienced certified public accountant, a Bible teacher, a speaker, a certified behavioral consultant specializing in understanding personality temperaments, and the author of *30 Days to Taming Your Tongue* and *Conquering Insecurity*. She and her husband, Darnell, have been married for more than 27 years and make their home in California.

For speaking engagements, please contact the author at:

> The Pegues Group
> P.O. Box 56382
> Los Angeles, California 90056
> (323) 293-5861

or

> E-mail: ddpegues@sbcglobal.net
> www.confrontingissues.com

Also by Deborah Smith Pegues
at www.confrontingissues.com:

Managing Conflict God's Way: Biblical Strategies for Effective Confrontations

30 Days to Taming Your Tongue

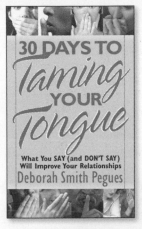

"I can't believe I just said that!"

Who hasn't struggled at times with saying the wrong thing at the wrong time? Certified behavioral consultant Deborah Pegues knows how easily a slip of the tongue can cause problems in personal and in business relationships. That is why she has put together a 30-day devotional to help you tame that unruly member and turn it into a productive asset. In this easy-to-read guide she discusses 30 negative speech patterns and offers effective methods to overcome them.

With humor and a bit of refreshing sass, Deborah devotes chapters to learning how you can overcome the

- Retaliating Tongue
- Hasty Tongue
- Know-It-All Tongue
- Gossiping Tongue
- Belittling Tongue
- And 25 more!

Short stories, anecdotes, soul-searching questions, and scripturally based personal affirmations combine to make each chapter tongue- and life-changing.

30 Days to Taming Your Stress

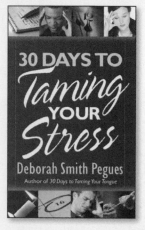

Are you sleeping well at night? Finding enough time in the day to do the things you enjoy? Making good choices about food and exercise? Sometimes stress causes us to miss out on the rest, fun, and health we long for. But you truly can tame this unruly taskmaster in 30 short days.

With insight gleaned from her experience as a behavioral consultant, bestselling author Deborah Smith Pegues devotes stress-free chapters to help you learn how to

- Change Self-Sabotaging Behavior • Enoy the Present
- Evaluate Your Expectations • Release Your Tension
- Solidify Your Support System • And 25 more!

Personal anecdotes, soul-searching questions, and biblical principles combine to make each chapter full of practical ways to help you stress less and enjoy life more in a remarkably short time.